FROM PROMISE
TO EXILE

THE FORMER PROPHETS

FROM PROMISE TO EXILE

THE FORMER PROPHETS

Marvin E. Tate

SMYTH&HELWYS
PUBLISHING, INCORPORATED • MACON, GEORGIA

Smyth & Helwys Publishing, Inc.
6316 Peake Road
Macon, Georgia 31210-3960
1-800-747-3016
©1999 by Smyth & Helwys Publishing
All rights reserved.
Printed in the United States of America.

Marvin E. Tate

The paper used in this publication meets the minimum requirements
of American National Standard for Information Sciences—
Permanence of Paper for Printed Library Materials.
ANSI Z39.48–1984. (alk. paper)

Unless otherwise indicated, all biblical quotations are taken from the
New Revised Standard Version (NRSV).

Library of Congress Cataloging-in-Publication Data

Tate, Marvin E.
    From promise to exile: the former prophets
    pp.   cm. —   (All the Bible)
    Includes bibliographical references.
    (alk. paper)
    1. Bible. O.T. Former Prophets—
    Criticism, interpretation, etc.
    I. Title.   II. Series.
    BS1286.5.T38   1999
    222'.06—dc21   99-39705
                         CIP
ISBN 1-57312-280-7

Contents

Introduction

How did the people of Israel go from inhabiting the promised land to living in a land of Exile, namely Babylon? How could they have received such a promise of new beginnings only to see it all taken away? This tragic story of rise and fall is found in Joshua–Kings. These books move from land, given as promised, to exile, executed by God (Yahweh) because of the infidelity of the people and the unwillingness of the kings to obey the Torah and listen to the prophets.

Why is it important to study about this odyssey from promised land to exile? A relevant reason is in the Near East. One can open almost any newspaper and see problems over land possession in Palestine and other areas. The Israeli-Palestinian question over who owns what land is not a recent issue. Indeed, both sides look to history to support their claims. A thorough study of Joshua–Kings can lead us to a fuller understanding of an issue that has extreme political and religious implications on an international scale. More, such a study ultimately reveals how religious believers can receive gifts from God that can be used appropriately, leading to reward, or inappropriately, leading to the loss of the gift itself.

Joshua, Judges, Ruth, 1 and 2 Samuel, and 1 and 2 Kings are historical books of the canon, but in Jewish tradition, except for Ruth, they are labeled as prophetic literature. In these books are some of the most familiar and unfamiliar stories in all of scripture: war and peace, birth and death, love and rape. In Joshua–Kings there are prophets, kings, and people called "judges," who are as different as Samson and Samuel, plus women who are as different as Deborah, Delilah, and Hannah.

These books describe the rise and fall of God's chosen people. What made them fall? What mistakes did they make? Did they do anything right? How strong was their faith? How strong is ours?

Divisions

I. Joshua

The successor of Moses leads the Israelites into settlement west of the Jordan River and toward possession of the land. Victories over the people in the land allow the allocation of portions of it to the tribes. At the end, Joshua makes a covenant between the people and Yahweh. On the whole, the accounts in Joshua are positive about Israel's success, but there are indications of incompleteness.

II. Judges

Settlement of the land is slow, followed by rebellion against Yahweh, oppression by non-Israelites, and then brief victories won by leaders called "judges." The efforts of the tribes to live successfully in the land go awry, and the narrative moves to a terrible end.

III. Samuel, Saul, David, and Solomon

Samuel, a Moses-type person, leads the tribes toward monarchy, which begins with Saul. The kingdom is established firmly by David and reaches maturation with Solomon. David captures Jerusalem from the Jebusites and makes it the capital of Israel, both politically and religiously. Solomon builds a temple in Jerusalem, and Yahwism is established as the official religion of Israel. The monarchy seems to hold great promise for Israel, but Solomon deserts the ideal.

IV. Two kingdoms

After the death of Solomon the kingdom divides into a northern kingdom—Israel, led by Jeroboam son of Nebat—and a southern kingdom—Judah, led by Rehoboam son of Solomon. The

Israelites are also divided religiously, but Yahwism and the traditions of Moses remain basic in both kingdoms. The 200-year division is marked by dynastic changes in the north versus continuation of the Davidic dynasty in the south; conflict between the kingdoms; major threats from external powers, especially the Arameans at Damascus and the Assyrians from northern Mesopotamia; and activity of prophets. It is through the prophets that God speaks to the kings and their people.

V. Judah Alone

Hezekiah and Josiah are exemplary kings, but Manasseh, Amon, Jehoiachim, Jehoiachin, and Zedekiah mar the history of the monarchy. Babylonia replaces Assyria as the dominant power, thrusting aside Egyptian efforts to rule in Palestine. After rebellions some people from Judah are deported to Babylonia in 597 BCE. Jerusalem and the temple are destroyed in 587–586, followed by more deportations. An attempt to establish a government under Gedaliah ends with his assassination by other Judeans, and some of the people travel to Egypt.

Language/Theology/History

I. Language

Except for Ruth, Joshua–Kings is very similar in language to the book of Deuteronomy. This is true especially in the sections that provide framing and comment for the content of the accounts (e.g., Josh 1; the prayer of Solomon in 1 Kgs 8:22-53; 2 Kgs 17:7-18). Thus, scholars commonly refer to Joshua–Kings as the Deuteronomistic History (Dtr, Dtrh, DH).

II. Theology

    A. Canaan is the promised land, or gift of Yahweh to Israel (Deut 6–8; Josh 1).

    B. Worship is centralized at one place—Jerusalem (Deut 12:4-7; 1 Kgs 11:13, 32, 36; 14:21; 2 Kgs 21:7; 23:27).

    C. Yahweh demands strict loyalty from the Israelites and prohibits worship of "other gods" (e.g., Deut 5:7; 6:14; 7:4; 8:19; 31:16-18; Josh 23:16; 24:16, Judg 2:12, 17, 19; 10:13; 1 Sam 8:8; 1 Kgs 9:6, 9; 11:4, 10; 2 Kgs 17:35, 37, 38).

   D. Israel is Yahweh's people (e.g., 1 Sam 12:22; 1 Kgs 8:16;
     16:2).
   E. Blessing and curse will come (Deut 28; Josh 23:14-16).
   F. Repentance is emphasized (Deut 4:25-31; 30:1-10; 1 Kgs
     8:33-36, 46-53; 2 Kgs 17:13; 23:25).

III. History/Author/Books

In Joshua–Kings the reader encounters the matter of the Bible
and history in a major way. These writings are frequently
referred to as historical books. However, one who tries to read
the content in terms of modern, critical history will be almost
constantly faced with problems. Gaps, discrepancies, and the
nature of the literature plague the reader intent on reconciling
the texts with external events, and indeed with themselves. The
content shifts back and forth between historical narrative and
legendary material with incomplete chronology (e.g,. see 1 Sam
13:1) and an exasperating lack of data. This is not to say that
the texts are entirely fiction or of no value historically. On the
contrary, they are of great worth, and the general nature of the
story they tell should not be doubted. Indeed, the narratives in
Joshua–Kings (and the parallels in Chronicles, some prophetic
books, and a few psalms) are the only source we have for much
of the history of Israel. There is no need for a deep separation
between textual content and historical questions.
    The reader needs to understand that Joshua–Kings is
intended to teach the meaning of Israel's history, meaning that
is always living and being expanded as one discovers new ways
to understand its events. Unless the reader wants to retreat to a
dogmatic position of no doubt, into some theory of strict biblical
inerrancy in which one is obligated to maintain the actual historical facticity of every report in the text, there must be some
coming to grips with the nature of history and history writing.
The formulation of history, in oral or written form, begins with
an interpreter who selects and arranges data (lists, genealogies,
chronologies, stories, reports, dates, physical artifacts, and the
like) into an account that makes sense. Thus history is always
an interpretation of data, formed by language, which cannot
exactly replicate the actual events—only approximate them.

History always has a subjective element; it always involves facts (data) and an interpreter and the context of the interpreter.

The modern critical historian works with significantly different assumptions and methods from ancient historians, such as those whose work we have in the Bible. The modern historian seeks as objective and probable reconstruction of the past as possible, using extensive documentation (usually written), along with physical artifacts, and striving to avoid bias or prejudice. There is concern for exact dates, names, causes, outcomes, and other data. Normally, God is not treated as a factor in historical events. Ancient historians often rely on both oral and written sources. They seem at times to have a dislike for precise facts and dates, showing primary interest in patterns and theological meaning. The style is frequently without detailed attention to a smoothly consistent account. In essence, the modern historian works to reconstruct events into a history without concern for message, whereas the ancient historian reconstructed events into a history of message.

The editor-writers intended to control the message through the formation of the historical accounts. However, the comparison should not be pushed too far. Ancient historians were also concerned about data, information, and intellectual honesty in telling the story of history. In one respect at least, they had an advantage over their modern counterparts in that they did not have to struggle with the "myth of uninterpreted history," or the idea that the primary purpose of historiography is to prepare a record of what actually happened free of presupposition and message.

Biblical interpretation has been plagued by the modern quest for certainty in historical study. The quest for certainty is misguided, however, and should be transferred to a quest for confidence and trust, along with a spirit of adventure as we try to learn more and understand better. The belief in certainty has become a modern myth that leads to skeptical relativism and holds nothing true, with everything depending upon point of view and with no real basis for evaluating conclusions: "It means whatever I want it to mean." Strangely enough, this is the curse of seeking certainty, the attempt to eliminate doubt, especially by sorting out and disposing of all legendary accretions in the accounts, which finally results in the loss of all certainty, or else leads to futile attempts to coerce certainty.

We are invited to live in the stories of Joshua–Kings until they become a part of our faith and of the way we live. We will ask the modern critical historical questions; we have no need to deny them, but we will not rest our faith on the answers, which will sometimes satisfy us and sometimes disturb us.

We do not know the identity of the person or persons who wrote Joshua–Kings. Some Jewish traditions ascribe authorship of Joshua in part to Joshua himself, but also recognizes that the book as we know it could not have been written by him because it records events after his death (1 Sam 25:1) and alleges that Eleazar and Phinehas completed the book. Samuel is given credit for writing Judges, Ruth, and Samuel. Of course, Samuel could not have written all of 1 and 2 Samuel because his death is recorded in 1 Samuel 25:1. In some traditions Jeremiah is said to have written Kings.

These traditional conclusions have little historical merit, except to indicate that the writing of the content of Joshua–Kings was accomplished in multiple stages over a long period of time and involving several writers. When we move beyond the diverse content of the different parts of Joshua–Kings, they appear to have been edited, or redacted, into a large literary complex known to scholars as the Deuteronomistic History (DH). DH is the work of one or more scribal editor-writers. The common conclusion today is that the shaping of the elongated and varied materials into a body of material with a broadly unified plan was accomplished in the exilic period about 550–540 BCE.

Some scholars argue strongly for two editor-writers of DH, one during the reign of Josiah (640–609 BCE) and a second about 550 BCE. Fortunately, absolute certainty about the issue of authorship and editorship is not crucial for reading Joshua–Kings, although it is important to ask questions about them. I am inclined to work with a single editor, but I suspect that the date is later than usually assumed. The place of writing is frequently taken to be Palestine among the people left behind after the exile. However, the ending of 2 Kings and other factors suggest a Babylonian context, and I see no strongly persuasive reason to reject it.

Purpose and Message

The basic purpose of Joshua–Kings is to explain to the Israelites, despite being given the land of Canaan by Yahweh, why the great disaster of the exile happened. It is intended to trace the history of Israel from land to exile and to demonstrate how the Israelites thwarted Yahweh's intention for them.

Theology in the ancient Near East centered on how each country/land had its own God. That God would give Israel a gift of land and take it away caused enormous doubt among the people in exile. Thus, the work is designed to show that Yahweh's actions are justified by the behavior of the people and their leaders, and also that the judgment is intentional on Yahweh's part—indeed, a demonstration of divine power. Yahweh gives land to possess to both Israel and other nations. Foreign kings and armies ultimately do the bidding of Israel's God; they have no legitimate right to possess land given to Israel by Yahweh, and their time there is limited if they are allowed to conquer it.

Joshua–Kings seems to have two other interests not explicitly stated. (1) It confirms the identity of the Israelites as the people chosen by Yahweh and the reliability of that choice, and (2) the pattern of judgment and deliverance points toward a new future beyond the uncertain ending of 2 Kings 25.

Joshua–Kings also raises the question as to whether or not Israel will remain as the people of Yahweh. This is the thrust of the disastrous end of Josiah's reign and the destruction of Jerusalem. Has the failure of the Davidic kings to do God's will brought an end to the Davidic dynasty, and thus brought an end to Yahweh's commitment to Israel?

There is no explicit answer, but the implicit answer is clearly negative: Yahweh will not allow the failure of the monarchy to end the divine mission for Israel. The Israelites were Yahweh's people before the monarchy, and there is good reason to believe that this relationship has not ended with the exile. The future of the monarchy is left unanswered, but Joshua–Kings is a harsh call for faith on the part of the people of God and a warning to the nations and their kings who think they rule the world.

For Further Reading

McKenzie, Steven L. "Deuteronomistic History." *The Anchor Bible Dictionary*. Edited by David Noel Freedman, et. al., 160-68. Volume 2. New York: Doubleday, 1992.

Noth, Martin. *The Deuteronomistic History*. Sheffield: JSOT Supp., 15, 1981, orig. ed. in German: 1943, 1957.

von Rad, Gerhard. *Old Testament Theology*. 2 vols. Translated by D. M. G. Stalker. New York: Harper & Row, 1962, 1965.

Well, Roy D., Jr. "Deuteronomic/Deuteronomistic Historian." *Mercer Dictionary of the Bible*. Edited by Watson E. Mills, et. al., 210-11. Macon GA: Mercer University Press, 1990.

Joshua

The book of Joshua follows the Pentateuch (Gen–Deut). A divine promise of land trails its way through the Pentateuch, but the promise is only partially fulfilled in Genesis–Deuteronomy. Moses is successful in settling 2½ tribes east of the Jordan, but he is only allowed to see the land of promise from the top of a mountain. Elaborate instructions for the Israelite possession of the land are found in Deuteronomy, but the actual possession is not described until we get to Joshua.

With the book of Joshua, the promise first given to Abraham and renewed with Moses and the Israelites at Mount Sinai is fulfilled. Moses was the leader of the exodus from Egypt, but Joshua is the leader when Israel takes possession of the land. The real chief character in the book, of course, is Yahweh, who directs and empowers events at every turn, with Joshua serving as the agent of divine power in history.

Despite Joshua's central role, from time to time he disappears from the action. He does not lead the Passover celebration (ch. 5), though he has prepared for it by circumcising the men. He does not initiate the action in 7:1, although he acts later to correct the situation. In 22:10-34 he is not directly involved in the action that results in a settlement of an altar dispute between the eastern and western tribes; Phinehas is the leader in this matter. The reason for Joshua's disappearance at places may be contextual. In the early chapters Joshua is not present at times of wrong action and withdraws in worship situations when a priest such as Phinehas has center stage. Nevertheless, his leadership frames the book in every major section.

Outline

I. Continuation of Moses' mission (1:1–12:24)

Joshua is commissioned as Moses' successor to carry out
the unfinished agenda regarding the promised land. The
account is framed by the commission of Joshua in 1:1-9
and by the summary in 11:23. Chapter 12 is an appendix.
The fulfillment of the mission to claim the promised land
is essential for the distribution of the land in chapters
13–21.

A. Commissioning of Joshua (1:1-9)

The land of promise is described in massive dimensions.
These are idealized boundaries probably drawn from the
actual extent of the Davidic empire at its maximum power.
The area exceeds that dealt with in Joshua 13–21 and
Judges 20:1.

  The use of the verb "give" is interesting. Verse 2 indicates that Yahweh is about to give the land; the divine
intention is to set the process in motion. Verse 3 points to
a decision already made; the divine decision may now be
implemented. It is time to go into the promised land.

B. Instructions for possessing the land (1:10-18)

Joshua commands the officers to instruct the people to
prepare to cross the Jordan and "take possession of the
land" (v. 11). Special attention is given to the tribes east of
the Jordan, who are not to be excused from the crossing
and the settlement on the West Bank. Indeed, their armed
men are to lead the way to the west and then return to
their lands and possessions east of the Jordan.

  Of major importance is the role of the *torah* (law) of
Moses in possessing the land. There is a strong emphasis
in Deuteronomistic theology on the divine gift of the land.
Yahweh's gift is not sheer gift, however. The "gifted" land
must be possessed by the Israelites and kept by Torah.

C. Rahab and the spies (2:1-24)

The story of Rahab is an independent narrative, linked to the fall of Jericho in chapter 6, but not directly related to chapters 3–5. Rahab, a non-Israelite, is remembered for her faith (Heb 11:31) and becomes an ancestor of Jesus (Matt 1:5). She is an exception among the peoples in the land who are supposed to be utterly destroyed by the Israelites.

D. Crossing the Jordan River (3:1–4:24)

The narrative of the location of Joshua and the Israelites at Shittim beyond the Jordan is resumed from 2:1. They camp by the Jordan for three days, at the end of which the officers and Joshua instruct the people and the priests about the crossing. They give orders to follow the ark of the covenant, which is to be carried by the priests at a safe distance from the people. The story of the crossing of the Jordan follows.

Three matters of a theological nature emerge from the narrative. The importance of the presence of Yahweh is stressed, with the divine presence focused on the ark of the covenant carried by the priests. The Israelites cross the Jordan on "dry ground," with the waters of the river "cut off," similar to the divine act at the sea during the exodus from Egypt. With the crossing, Yahweh has already deprived the inhabitants of the land of their courage.

E. Ceremonies at Gilgal (5:2-12)

Circumcision is instituted for the males of Israel, emphasizing readiness for acceptance of the divine calling and its obligations in the land. The old way of life is "cut off," and they are ready for the new. Verses 2-9 assume that the males who came out of Egypt were circumcised, but that the males born to the new generation in the wilderness were not.

The celebration of Passover at Gilgal is recounted in verses 10-12. The observance is not described in detail, but the emphasis seems to be twofold. Explicitly, the observance of Passover marks the end of the wilderness period and the time of feeding on the manna supplied by Yahweh. They could now eat "the produce of the land . . . the crops of the land of Canaan" (v. 12). Implicitly, the celebration marks the conclusion of the Exodus and the fulfillment of the promise of the land.

F. Capture of Jericho (5:13–6:27)

A prologue to the account of Jericho's fall tells of the "commander of the army of the Lord" appearing to Joshua near Jericho. Perhaps we should think of Joshua looking over the terrain as he prepares to attack the city. Although it is closed tightly against invaders, Joshua is given divine assurance that it has already been handed over to him. The divine verdict on Jericho is operative; its fate is already certain (see 2:24).

The phrase "devoted to destruction" (6:18, 21), sometimes translated as "utterly destroyed" or "put under the ban" (KJV, "accursed thing"), is an attempt to translate the Hebrew word *herem*, which appears in noun and verb forms. The term carries two basic connotations: forbidden and sacred. When used in war or warlike contexts, the concept is that of total destruction of a condemned people and their property because the people and property are devoted to God. Rahab and her family are spared by Joshua's orders.

The story of the fall and capture of Jericho is one of the most famous of the Bible. Israelite warriors circle the walls for six days. The warriors lead the way, followed by seven priests blowing horns and going ahead of the ark. A rear guard comes behind the ark. The people as a whole do not seem to participate in the daily circumvention of the walls; their mission is to wait silently for the long blast on the ram's horn and the sound of the trumpet before giving a great shout and charging into the city when the walls fall (6:5, 9-10, 16, 20). On the seventh day the procession circles the walls seven times. On the seventh time the priests blow a signal on the horns; Joshua commands the people to shout, and the wall falls (6:20). The people then charge into the city to take possession of it (6:20-21).

G. Defeat and victory at Ai (7:1–8:29)

Achan takes some of the banned things at Jericho, and the "anger of the Lord burns against the Israelites." Disaster is sure to follow; the Israelites are in serious trouble.

In its first part the narrative is another spy story. Joshua sends spies from Jericho to reconnoiter the land in the area of Ai, but without any authorization from Yahweh. Their overconfident report results in a relatively small corps of troops going up to attack Ai. The result is a disastrous defeat. Ironically, "the hearts of the people melt and turn to water," a condition their enemies previously experienced (2:11; 5:1).

The remainder of chapter 7 is concerned with the ferreting out of Achan from among the tribes, clans, and families of the Israelites as the guilty person who is responsible for their defeat. Achan confesses to taking a mantle, 200 shekels of silver, and a 50-shekel bar of gold. His act has put all the people in danger.

The interrelatedness/corporate nature of life is strongly focused here. Yahweh's message to Joshua is: "Israel has sinned; they have transgressed my covenant" (v. 11), although only the action of one man is involved. To remove the virus of sin from the community, Achan is stoned to death, and then he and his children and all his property—including the booty taken from Jericho—are burned in the Valley of Achor. Note, "all Israel" is involved with Achan's death. To mark the spot of Achan's death, they raise a heap of stones and name the area the Valley of Achor, meaning "Valley of Trouble." This chapter ends with a famous note: "The Lord turned from his burning anger."

After the story of Achan, the narrative returns to another expedition against the town of Ai. Joshua organizes the attack against Ai at divine command, in contrast to chapter 7 where he sends out spies on his own authority, and with only partial involvement of the people. This attack is successful.

H. Building an altar; reading the Torah (8:30-35)

In accordance with the commands of Moses, Joshua builds an altar on Mount Ebal. The reference to Moses' instruction (*torah*) seems to relate to passages from Deuteronomy (11:29-30; 27–28).

I. Covenant with the Gibeonites (9:1-27)

The account of the Gibeonites has three parts: their plan to gain a treaty with the Israelites (vv. 3-15); the Israelite discovery of the scheme and the reaction of the leaders of the congregation (vv. 16-21); and Joshua's address to them with a summary of his actions (vv. 22-27).

J. Victories in the south (10:1-43)

The covenant with the Gibeonites brings about a major movement by five city-state kings against Gibeon, a large city in which all the men are warriors. The Gibeonites appeal for help to Joshua and the Israelites, their new covenant partners. Joshua and his forces march overnight from Gilgal. Encouraged by a word from Yahweh, they put the forces of the kings to flight, assisted by a panic thrown into them by Yahweh and a mighty hailstorm, which kills more "than the Israelites kill with the sword" (v. 11). Despite their attempts to escape, the five kings are destroyed by Joshua. Their bodies are hanged on five trees, a great disgrace and representative of a curse by God.

A different type of material is found in the account of Joshua's campaign in the south. The terse narrative, using stereotypical expressions, is in the "daybook style" used by Egyptians to record military campaigns. Joshua applied the ban to all the cities and their kings. The brief summary of the southern conquests stresses the completeness of Joshua's efforts ("the whole land"—"at one time"), his obedience to the command of Yahweh, and the fact that "the Lord God fought for Israel."

K. Victories in the north (11:1-15)

The Israelites and a coalition of northern kings, led by King Jabin of Hazor, go to battle at "the waters of Merom." Then Joshua turns away from the victory there and attacks and destroys Hazor, about seven or eight miles away. Other towns in the area are attacked and conquered, but they are not burned as is Hazor. The ban ("utterly destroy") is enforced so far as human beings are concerned ("they did not leave any who breathed," v. 14), but the Israelites are allowed to take spoil and livestock from the towns.

L. Joshua's conquests (11:16–12:24)

The remainder of chapter 11 and all of chapter 12 are a mixed collection of material, probably taken from different traditions. The section concludes the account of Joshua's taking the promised land and prepares for the accounts of the division of land among the tribes in the following chapters.

A general geographical resume, covering the territory from south to north, and an account of the extermination of the Anakim are given (11:16-20). However, some Anakim survive in the Philistine cities of Gaza and Ashdod. They appear to have lived in Palestine before the Israelites and are believed to be giants.

Verse 23 is a summary statement of the achievement of Joshua in taking the whole land, adding that he has given it as Israel's inheritance in the form of tribal allotments, and that the land has "rest from war." The verse affirms that Joshua has completed what he was charged to do and provides a transition to chapters 13–19.

Chapter 12 ends with a list of conquered kings: those east of the Jordan (12:1-6) and those west of the Jordan (12:7-24).

II. Distribution of the promised land (chs. 13–23)

While the following chapters are considered by many to be dry and unimportant, the allocation of the land to the tribes is the fulfillment of the promise made by God to the Israelites. The conquest may have been sporadic at best, but the end result was that God's promise came to be.

Chapters 13–23 are difficult to read because they contain many names, lists of towns, and boundary descriptions. Some narrative material is found, however, namely vignettes that portray various features of the settlement of the tribes east and west of the Jordan. The section is framed by a prologue (13:1-7) and Joshua's speech (ch. 23), both of which are concerned with the advanced age of Joshua and with the nations that remain in the land. The possession of the land involves much more than the great victories of chapters 1–12. Military-type successes only open doors to possess the land, which must be done tribe by tribe, and even family by family, in obedience to Yahweh and in a program outlined by Moses.

One of the major features of chapters 13–23 is that of the difference between the land actually possessed and the land promised. The references to unpossessed territory are numerous. The allocation of territory is made despite the fact that possession of the land is incomplete in major areas and represents an act of faith.

In 18:1 the site for land allocation suddenly changes from Gilgal to Shiloh, a major worship center. The statement that "the land lay subdued before them" recalls Genesis 1:28, linking Joshua and the Pentateuch and indicating Israel's role in God's plan to "fill the earth and subdue it."

According to the proposed plan of Moses, cities of refuge are designated by Joshua (20:1-9), and cities are assigned to the Levites (21:1-42). The cities of refuge are intended to provide justice and remove the loss of life because of family vengeance. It is doubtful that any such system of asylum cities ever actually operated in Israel; the accounts are expressive of idealized conditions.

The long narrative in chapter 22 tells the story of a huge altar constructed by the Transjordan tribes on their way home from Shiloh. The altar is built on the west side of the Jordan in the territory of the other tribes. The West Jordan tribes are greatly disturbed by the altar and gather at Shiloh to prepare to go to war against the Transjordan tribes. Before going to war, however, they send Phinehas, a priest and son of Eleazar, with leaders of the tribes to negotiate the matter. Phinehas and his group are successful. All parties agree the altar is not to be used for any kind of sacrifice, but is to be a witness of unity between the two groups of tribes. The West Bank tribes accept the claim of the Transjordan tribes that they have built a no-sacrifice altar and their promise to keep it that way, thus desisting from their plans for war.

III. Covenant at Shechem; sending people to their inheritances (24:1-28)

Chapter 24 has received a great deal of attention from Old Testament scholars because of its unusual content, especially that dealing with the making of a covenant. The ceremony relates to prior material (8:30-35) and shows Joshua acting in obedience to the commands of Moses (Deut 11; 27; 31). Verses 1-28 may belong to an originally independent body of Shechem traditions, now added to show that all Israel is united in the worship of Yahweh.

IV. Three burials (24:29-33)

The burial notices bind the book of Joshua to the Pentateuch and also link Joshua to the book of Judges (see the account of the death of Joshua in Judg 2:6-10).

A. Joshua (24:29-31)

There is an obvious parallel between the ending of Deuteronomy (ch. 34) with the death of Moses and the ending of the book of Joshua with a notice of the death of Joshua. Like Moses, Joshua is now called a "servant of the Lord" (v. 29), whereas earlier he was referred to as "Moses' assistant." His life span of 110 years is the same as that of Joseph, but ten years less than that of Moses. His burial place, Timnath-serah, is on land granted to him at the end of the allocation to all Israel, located in the hill country of Ephraim. Although its precise location is unknown, it is inside the land, not outside, as in the case of Moses.

B. Joseph (24:32)

Joseph's bones are buried in the promised land in a portion of ground bought by Jacob at Shechem, the original burial place. The work of Moses, who had brought the bones out of Egypt, is finished (see Gen 50:25; Exod 13:19). All ancestors are buried in the promised land. The Exodus is complete, and the settlement in the land is bound to the promises of the past. The burial of Joseph's remains binds together the Pentateuch with Joshua.

C. Eleazar (24:33)

Eleazar, son of Aaron and father of Phinehas, is buried at a place in Ephraim. In Old Testament accounts, Eleazar is linked with the closing work of both Moses and Joshua (Num 26:63; 27:22; 31:12, 18-25, 31; Josh 14:1).

Commentary and Reflection

I. Historical problems

The book of Joshua is replete with questions of history. For example, questions relating to the conquest of Ai and Jericho have been the subjects of extensive discussion. The archaeological evidence from both of these sites is difficult to harmonize with the biblical accounts.

Jericho was an ancient city, dating to 9000 BCE. It was located on a fertile plain about six miles north of the Dead Sea. The mound that marks the site today is about 70 feet high and covers about 10 acres. At various times in its history Jericho had large protective walls, but most recent excavations reveal no trace of walls during the time of Joshua.

The location of Ai is commonly identified with the modern site of et-Tell, near Bethel on the east side. The site is in the hill country well above the location of ancient Jericho in the Jordan Valley. Ai means "ruin" or literally in the Hebrew text "The Ruin," which accounts for the play on the meaning of the name in 8:28. Archaeological evidence indicates Ai was once a massive fortified town, but then lay in ruins for many years before reoccupation. In any case, the data does not correlate well with the stories in Joshua 7 and 8. Ai cannot be definitively located in time nor space. Fortunately, the power of these stories does not depend on historical precision.

II. The long day and miracle

The "miracle" is focused on 10:12-14, which is part of the narrative of Joshua's campaign in the south against the five kings of the Amorites. The sun and moon are implored not to shine or to stand still without moving. The prayer is for either the continuation or the establishment of conditions favorable for victory. However, the text is obscure as to the benefit to be gained by the movement of the sun and moon.

If the request is for the sun and moon not to shine and let the early morning darkness continue, augmented by the blackness of a severe thunderstorm, the request could be understood as one for the continuation of the conditions in verses 9-11, with verse 13 affirming that this happened. Ancient Near Eastern texts relating to the sun and moon in times of war indicate that when the sun arises in the east shortly before the moon sets in the west, it is an omen that can be favorable if it occurs on the first day of the new moon, but unfavorable if it occurs on other days. Did Joshua want a favorable sign for the Israelites? Or did he want an unfavorable sign for the Amorites? In any case, the sun and moon responded so that the Israelites "took vengeance on their enemies" (v. 13).

Keep in mind that poetic enhancement of the meteorological and human events of the day presents scientific difficulties. We have questions: What happened to the moon? Did the moon stop when the sun stopped? Verse 14a seems to refer to a "miracle" day that exceeds any confluence of events, natural and human, and the account has frequently been read as the report of an extraordinary cosmic event. The reporting of a cosmic "miracle" of unprecedented proportions is not intended, however, although the text sets forth a "long day."

Joshua 10 provides a good context for a brief reflection on the nature of biblical miracles. However, it is difficult to draw positive conclusions about biblical miracles for several reasons. First, neither the Old Testament nor the New Testament has a word that is directly equivalent to the English word "miracle."

Both testaments, of course, use a cluster of words for extraordinary events that we might term "miracle." In the Old Testament one finds "great things" and "signs and wonders." The New Testament has a similar range of words. In biblical usage a "sign" or "wonder" may refer to an event that could be called a "miracle," but also to events normally considered natural. The key idea is that "signs and wonders" are indicators of the presence of God in special ways, ways that may appear miraculous or as ordinary phenomena such as a rainbow.

Second, it is very difficult to establish the validity of a miracle. The biblical material is informed by a worldview that includes the continuing work of divine power. The line between a miracle and a natural event is blurred. Thus, God is an active agent in the contingency of both human and nonhuman existence. In biblical thought, God is always engaged with both history and creation. Creation has not been delivered to immutable law, which is simply allowed to run its course. Therefore, the biblical worldview makes "miracle" (in the sense of a suspension of the laws of nature) problematical. The concept of natural law is a modern one and foreign to the Bible. All law is God's law, natural or historical, so that an either-or alternative in regard to miracles is false from the biblical view.

Furthermore, the recognizably complex ecology of the world precludes absolute certainty about miracles. The line between natural and supernatural is not clear. We can know that extraordinary things happen, but it seems foolish to claim too quickly that they are miracles, unless everything God does is miracle. The concurrence of normal factors and events may be natural and a stunning display of divine energy at the same time. Religious life is plagued by those who claim to be the recipients of miracles and who are intent on telling everyone about them. Surely, the sense of divine presence, extraordinary divine energy, and miracles should engender humility, thanksgiving, and renewed dedication to service. Boasting about miracles is an abomination and is often based on false assessment.

Third, we must allow for the poetic nature of many biblical accounts. Poetry is characterized by the use of enhanced, figurative language, which is frequently metaphorical. Poetic features are essential in reporting phenomena that manifest transcendent dimensions, at least for those "who have eyes to see and ears to hear." Some events only make sense when a poet takes them out of the ordinary and transmutes them into forms we may call legendary or mythical.

All of this seems to point toward a nondogmatic approach to biblical "miracles." On the one hand, the "available believable" should be kept wide, but we should not draw back from critical evaluation. The wise will reserve judgment about what really happened, which in any case is beyond the human capacity to know in an absolute sense. Testimony should be marked by thanksgiving-praise and fixed on results without dogmatic affirmations of what really happened or on claims of special favors by God. In other words, the wise will say, "I don't know why this happened to me, but I receive it gratefully and use it to renew and empower my faith in God."

III. Covenant

The central event of 24:1-28 is the covenant made by Joshua for the people. The covenant, of course, is one made between Yahweh and the people, although Joshua acts as Yahweh's agent.

The concept of covenant is basic in biblical thought. The basic idea refers to a binding relationship of mutual obligation and/or commitment between persons or parties. Joshua made statutes and ordinances for Israel, which he wrote "in the book of the law of God." The obligation assumed by Yahweh is set forth in the great story of God's saving deeds (24:2-13, 16-18).

The Israelites seem to have adapted the treaty covenant to conceptualize their relationship with Yahweh. In this form a strong king would make a treaty with a vassal of lesser power and resources. The king assumed obligation for the protection and welfare of the vassal, sometimes recalling a history of benevolent actions toward the vassal. Stipulations were spelled out for the behavior of the vassal, with special emphasis on loyalty. These treaties were written in two or more copies and carefully preserved. Witnesses were appealed to for the verification and enforcement of the treaty. The witnesses were usually gods who would see that the curses of disobedience and the blessings of obedience would be operative.

In Old Testament contexts, there can be no appeal to other gods. Thus, Joshua sets up a permanent stone under an oak tree in the area of the sanctuary as a witness. Other elements of the treaty covenant form are obvious: the benevolent history; the stipulations; and the intense demand for commitment and loyalty on the part of Israel, who must choose between the gods of their ancestors, the gods of the land in which they are living, and Yahweh. The people make their choice: "The Lord our God we will serve, and him we will obey" (24:24).

IV. Hardening the heart

The "hardening of hearts" by divine action in 11:20 is one of the more troubling aspects of biblical theology. The expression used is found elsewhere only with reference to the Egyptian Pharaoh whom Moses confronted in Exodus 1–15. The "hardened heart" refers to a stubborn and unyielding will. In 11:20 Yahweh is said to have set the will of the opposing kings on battle so that they would attack Israel and be "utterly destroyed" and exterminated without mercy. In both Joshua and Exodus, Yahweh is dealing with obstinate kings, set on having their way in the world and on destroying the Israelites. One of the weapons Yahweh uses against them is hardened hearts, so that the intensity of their opposition is increased to such a degree as to preclude any deliverance from the terrible consequences of their actions. Of course, the kings can harden their own hearts, as did the Pharaoh, but once their wills are set on resistance to the divine will, their mind-set is boosted by divine power in order to wreak their destruction.

In interpreting this feature of divine action, keep in mind that the kings represent the rulers and authorities (Eph 6:12) who allow themselves to be used as leaders of rebellion against the will of God. This is clearer in the plague passages in Exodus than in Joshua. The Pharaoh of Egypt was considered as almost god incarnate, the ruler of a great empire belonging to the gods he served. Such "powers" threaten the order of divine creation with the chaos of violence and injustice. The texts in Joshua are not so explicit, but there can be little doubt that the kings are considered to be agents of evil. Thus, the action of Yahweh is not directed toward ordinary mortal sinners, but toward superhuman beings who conspire and plot against the Lord (Ps 2:2).

Also remember that a balance should be maintained between divine determination of purpose and the response of human will. In the case of the Egyptian king and the plagues, the will of Yahweh for the liberation of the people is firm. Similarly, in Joshua, Yahweh's intention to give the promised land to Israel is a nonnegotiable act.

The same resoluteness of purpose should not be read into the hardening of hearts, however. Its purpose in Joshua is to facilitate the divine decision regarding the land. In the case of the Egyptian Pharaoh, the heart hardening is not all a divine business; the king and his officials are cooperative subjects. Moses and Aaron present the Pharaoh with the option of obedience or disobedience, and the Pharaoh's officials advise him to let the Israelites go; thus, the divine hardening does not override the king's decision-making powers.

V. The land

According to Walter Brueggemann (*The Land*), land is a central theme of biblical faith and theology. He notes that the Israelites are without a place of their own in three contexts: as sojourners in the ancestor narratives, as wanderers in the wilderness narratives, and as exiles after the destruction of the Temple and the loss of land in Palestine. In all these contexts, however, the promise of land is operative; they anticipate going to the land either for the first time or else returning to it.

There are differences in land theology, but some major features are either explicit or implicit in all the material. First, Yahweh is the landowner of the world who allocates a part of the universal domain to Israel and also determines the assignments of kings, nations, and peoples to land. This concept is rooted in the ancient thought that ultimately kings owned their lands and had the right to use them as sources of wealth. The deities of each reign guaranteed both the monarch's right to rule and his/her entitlement to the land and the people who lived on it. Thus, it is Yahweh who "gives" land to Israel, and in doing so strips the land away from the kings who have owned it.

Second, Israel's land is allocated according to divine will for use as the chosen people of Yahweh in the world. Israel does not own the land by any kind of inherent right, and the gift of land is contingent on Israel's proper possession of it. In other words, Israel cannot do with the land as it pleases; the land is held in trust by the action of the divine landowner.

Closely related to Israel's possession of the land is the idea that Yahweh shares the land with Israel; it is God's property, and God is the divine custodian. Indeed, the land designated for Israel has superlative quality (see Jer 3:19); it is a "land of milk and honey" (Exod 3:8). Yahweh intented for the land of Israel and for the whole world of human habitation to be a huge Garden of Eden, shared with the divine presence, with lush fertility and well-being for all. (See Lev 26:4-6, 11-12).

Third, Israel's claim to the land is contingent. The Old Testament is replete with divine warnings regarding the loss of fertility and productivity. Israel must possess the land by obedience to the will of Yahweh and by not polluting its holiness.

Note that much of the account of Israel involves landlessness and exile. The fundamental charter of Israelite life deals with a people without land, an Israel who lives out of the promise of land. Israel becomes a nation and develops its basic institutions during the bondage in Egypt and in the wilderness. After the destruction of the kingdoms, Israel lives as a people divided between land and exile. Exodus, wilderness, and exile, these make it clear that land is not of ultimate meaning. Israel is the people of Yahweh before the gift of land and does not cease to be so in exile.

Other observations concerning the land are also worth noting. For example, both "land" and "earth" are used, the borders of Israel are never precisely defined, and such basic institutional ceremonies as Passover and Sabbath do not depend on being in the land. To some degree, all this prepares us for the strong downgrading of the emphasis on land in the New Testament. The land theology of the Old Testament is dissolved in various New Testament passages and transformed into a theology of the whole earth. The holy land of Israel is now the world, and God's presence is found wherever the people of faith dwell.

Place, space, land, and living room are of universal significance for all humanity. Land and place are essential for personal identity and health. Human beings and nonhuman animals need spatial identity and security, familiar areas where there can be free movement to meet survival needs, physical and

spiritual. The loss of a sense of land and place is a major problem of modern urban life. According to Brueggemann, a sense of
place is a human hunger unmet by urban life. Thus, the New
Testament imagery of a new heaven and a new earth, or a New
Jerusalem in the Garden of Eden, offers hope and substance.

VI. The divine choice of Israel

Yahweh's choice of Israel is traditionally known as "the election
of Israel." Throughout the Old Testament the emphasis is on
God's choosing, or divine action, rather than on a status
assumed by the elect. Israel is referred to as God's "treasured
possession," "a people holy," "my people," and "called by name."

The very concept of a divinely chosen people is difficult to
accept. Many modern people would consider it unfair and arbi-
trary for God to choose a particular people as a way to redeem
all peoples. Too often election has been interpreted by those who
understand themselves as among the elect as privilege and
special honor. The elect are always tempted to yield to the urge
to fence off themselves from the rest of the world and promote
intolerance. However, careful adherence to the biblical material
relating to election can clarify and undergird the doctrine with
healthy understanding.

There is mystery, of course, in the ways of God, and we
cannot penetrate into the full nature of the divine decision to
choose Israel. The biblical material itself grounds the decision
for Israel in Yahweh's love for a weak people and in the promise
made to their ancestors. Theologian Wolfhart Pannenberg
(*Human Nature, Election, and History*) points to three major
elements in the classical doctrine of election, as represented in
the work of Augustine, Thomas Aquinas, and John Calvin:

• the timelessness of the divine decision in regard to its subject
• the restriction of its objects to individuals
• the purpose as predominantly that of ultimate salvation

However, the biblical material runs counter to all three of
these tenets. First, election in the biblical texts is predominantly
historical, not eternal and timeless. Yahweh's choice of Israel is
made in the context of human and nonhuman history. The
contingent nature of election means that deterministic interpre-

tations of divine action are put under great stress. Theologians frequently try to move out of this bind by shifting the action of election to some pre-creation or eternal mode and/or by trying to hide behind a hyperparadox, which harmonizes a static nature of God with human freedom and the uncertainties of actual life. The result is often the reduction of human freedom to a divine charade and/or paradox, pushed to the point of nonsense. The Bible urges us to live with the uncomfortable reality of the nature of God.

Second, election is primarily corporate and communal in nature. Even in individual cases a communal context is clear. In the New Testament, individuals are chosen "in Christ," who is the locus of the election work of God.

The third major facet of divine election is that of its nature as an assignment to mission. Election by Yahweh gives Israel the status of a monarch's treasured possession. Israel is a holy people, separated from the ordinary population of the world as "a kingdom of priests." Israel is like God's "firstborn" son (Exod 4:22-23).

Along with the privilege as God's chosen, however, come responsibility and service. Israel is chosen for God's divine purpose in the world, and cannot live as other nations do; it must be different. Israel is to be a servant, called to live under divine discipline, to suffer, and to wait for the deliverance of God. Election always means mission, and the elect are accountable to God for assigned work.

Finally, election involves the threat of failure. God intends the divine choice of people to be permanent, but the elect may become candidates for rejection; election may be nullified. The warnings of both Testaments should be taken seriously. Even the elect on the way to the promised land may die in the wilderness (see Heb 3:7-19), but Yahweh is incredibly persistent in enduring love by pursuing the wayward people through history like a hound of heaven, intent that they will not be forever lost.

VII. War

The prevalence of war and war-related actions in the Joshua-Kings narratives forces the reader to reflect on some vexing questions:

- Why is there so much violence and war involved with the people of God?
- Why is Yahweh presented as a divine warrior who accomplishes major objectives by the use of war?
- How are we to relate to this kind of biblical content?
- Does the Bible give us authority to use violence and wage war?

The answers to these questions may seem easy to the Christian who remembers that God is loving; who recalls that Jesus was a person of nonviolence who was crucified without forceful resistance, praying for the forgiveness of his crucifiers, blessing the peacemakers, teaching us to love our enemies. But our knowledge of Christ's life and teachings raises important questions when studied in the context of Old Testament history. For example, how can we reconcile the example and teachings of Christ with the Old Testament vision of Yahweh as a terrible divine warrior with arms bared against the enemy? Is the God who commanded Israel to fight and kill their enemies, who destroyed the Egyptians in the sea, the Father of our Lord Jesus Christ?

There are no easy answers for this matter, but in general, the Old Testament treats war as a given, a fact of life, an institution common to human societies, and one that God sometimes uses for divine purposes. However, there is diversity as to how the people of Yahweh are to relate to war.

The biblical content dealing with war and violence is complex. In the beginning, creation focuses on worship and an ideal society free of chaos and violence. In the ancestor narratives in Genesis, war elements are minor. Even in instances of defeat of the enemy, mercenary intent is renounced. Troublemakers are frowned upon. In some traditions even the occupation of the promised land appears as a peaceful process, without great violence.

The concentration on war is found mainly in certain sections of Genesis–Numbers and in Deuteronomy–Kings. Here we find the laws of war and the ideology of possessing the land by armed invasion. The Israelites are to drive out the peoples of the land and dispossess them of their property. The application of the ban and the use of military power to form and sustain the life of the Israelite state are set forth. Thus there is an intertextual tension between those parts of Genesis–Kings that present a picture of peaceful occupation of the land with life in the land as a worshiping community without war, and those parts that either treat war as a natural element of society or consider the concept of holy war to be foundational for the existence of Israel.

Militaristic aspects of war in the Old Testament include the function of Yahweh as divine warrior who goes out to confront enemies who threaten the well-being of the world and of Israel. Yahweh is depicted as garbed in armor and possessing weapons for battle, smiting foes and saving Israel. Returning victoriously to the holy place, Yahweh is hailed as the King of Glory, strong and mighty in battle (Ps 24). Some portrayals are even expressed in terms of ferocious violence, as in destruction of certain places. The emphasis is on the motif of victory—or defeat—as due to Yahweh alone. Israelite warriors may go to war, but the warrior who counts is Yahweh.

Sometimes the divine warrior opposes the chosen people if they disobey the divine will and are disloyal to Yahweh. One form of this action is Yahweh's refusal to go out with the Israelites to battle, which brings about their defeat. Or Yahweh may fight against the Israelites and with their enemies. Or Yahweh may use foreign powers to punish the chosen people.

The warrior is also creator and divine king. The concept of a deity as divine king-warrior was widespread in the ancient Near East and was associated with battle, or struggle, to create and maintain order in the cosmos. War is a form of chaos that threatens the created order. As the divine warrior, Yahweh will not always tolerate or use the chaotic power of war. Thus, Yahweh is portrayed as the divine peacemaker who will eventually destroy the weapons of war and bring the people to a life of rest, peace, and well-being. The hostile forces of chaos and war are charged to "be still and know that I am God" (Ps 46:10). Yahweh will ultimately destroy the weapons of Israel and its enemies, establishing a demilitarized world that lives in peace.

The nations of the world have, of course, been extremely reluctant to move toward a time when war is "learned no more"—and if war is "learned," it has to be "taught." The teaching of war has been a major business of humankind, often led by Christians who convert the cross into a sword and the love of God into hatred of the enemy, and who support "ethnic cleansing" and the "purity of the church" ostensibly for the glory of God. However, the domination system of greed, violence, war, exploitation, and aggression is not eternal. God is moving the world toward an era of a domination-free order; the divine objective is the redemption of the domination system so that we learn and teach war no more.

I will conclude this discussion with some words I wrote several years ago for the *Review and Expositor*:

> War is a dreadful evil and a scourge of humanity. If a Jew or a Christian does participate in war, it ought always to be with a heavy heart and a sense of deep failure, knowing full well that the mission of the people of Yahweh should be that of peacemakers and not warriors. On the other hand, we ought not to try to banish the Divine Warrior from our theological heritage. He has used war to accomplish his purposes in history—at times against his own people—and he may do so again. We dare not make absolutes out of either violence or nonviolence, war or peace. But our mission is clear; we are to move toward the vision of justice and peace which the Divine Warrior has given to his people. For the Divine Warrior is also our loving heavenly Father, the Father of our Lord Jesus Christ.

Conclusion

Deuteronomy 34 with its account of Moses' death forms a definite break between the Pentateuch and the book of Joshua. The separation is enhanced by the uniqueness ascribed to Moses, whom Yahweh "knew face to face." None was like him in Israel as a prophet and as one who did the signs and wonders of Yahweh in Egypt, displays of power done in the sight of Israel. Clearly, Moses is to have no duplicate personhood in Israel. Nevertheless, the book of Joshua is an integral complement of the Pentateuch, especially in regard to the great promise of peoplehood and land. It contains the story of how Israel came to be fully established in the promised land. The covenant between Yahweh and Israel made at Sinai-Horeb, and renewed at the border by Moses, is now established with all Israel in the land.

The book of Joshua is most commonly read as history, and most interpretations of the book concentrate on historical issues. This is regrettable because it ignores the many ethical and theological issues in it. The notes and reflections in the material above have given brief attention to some of these matters. Space excludes a full discussion of the questions and subjects, but one subject requiring attention is a matter of faith. The book of Joshua is a testimony to the ways of God that are not our ways. No one who reads the initial promise of peoplehood and land in Genesis 12:1-3 can envision from that text its fulfillment in the book of Joshua. God does divine work in the world in God's own ways, which never cease to be surprising.

For Further Reading

Auld, A. Graeme. *Joshua, Judges, and Ruth.* The Daily Study Bible Series. Philadelphia: Westminster, 1984.

Boling, Robert G., and G. Ernest Wright. *Joshua.* The Anchor Bible. New York: Doubleday, 1982.

Butler, Trent C. *Joshua.* Word Biblical Commentary. Waco TX: Word Books, 1983.

_____. *Understanding the Basic Themes of Joshua.* Dallas: Word Publishers, 1991.

Coogan, Michael David. "Joshua." *The New Jerome Commentary.* Edited by Raymond E. Brown, Joseph A. Fitzmyer, and Roland E. Murphy, 110-31. Englewood Cliffs NJ: Prentice Hall, 1990.

Curtis, Adrian H. W. *Joshua.* The Old Testament Library. Sheffield: Sheffield Academic Press, 1994.

Fewell, Donna Nolan. "Joshua." *The Women's Bible Commentary.* Edited by Carol A. Newsom and Sharon H. Ringe, 63-66. Louisville KY: Westminster/John Knox, 1992.

Laughlin, John C. H. "Joshua." *Mercer Commentary on the Bible.* Edited by Watson E. Mills, et al., 227-41. Macon GA: Mercer University Press, 1995.

Nelson, Richard D. *Joshua: A Commentary.* The Old Testament Library. Louisville KY: Westminster/John Knox, 1997.

Polzin, Robert. *Moses and the Deuteronomist,* 73-145. New York: Seabury, 1980.

Soggin, J. Alberto. *Joshua: A Commentary.* The Old Testament Library. Translated by R. A. Wilson. Philadelphia: Westminster, 1972.

Tate, Marvin. "War and Peacemaking in the Old Testament." *Review and Expositor,* LXXIX (1982): 592-93, 94-95.

Judges

Following the death of Joshua, the book of Judges is a literary mosaic of stories and episodes about life in Canaan between the incomplete conquest and the rise of the monarchy. Moses and Joshua are no longer available to lead the tribes. Like the exodus generation of the Israelites who died in the wilderness, the generation who crossed the Jordan into the promised land dies in the midst of unfinished work. With no Moses or Joshua, the "judges" will now provide some leadership, but the enterprise will still fail to accomplish the purpose of properly possessing the land.

The stories in Judges represent a pattern for life in Israel between promise and exile. The people forsake Yahweh, worship other gods, fall into the hands of an enemy, and call out for Yahweh's help. Yaheweh raises a deliverer to liberate them from their plight. This pattern continues in one form or another throughout the books of Joshua, Judges, Samuel, and Kings. At the end of Kings, however, there is no real freedom—only exile and limited hope for the future. Joshua–Kings wait for a more definite word of God's future for Israel.

Generally, the book of Judges deals with high hopes and great potential that fade into weakness and violence. It struggles with the question of Israel's uncertain future. Can life in the land be sustained with patterns of negative, unbelieving behavior exhibited in these narratives? The book provides a rationale for monarchy with the repeated observation that "in those days there was no king in Israel." This expression at the end of the book is matched by the declaration that "all the people did what was evil in their own eyes" (21:25), violating the commandment requiring absolute loyalty to Yahweh. Can they possess the land?

Outline

I. Reprise of the conquest and settlement of the land (1:1–3:6)

A. Prologue I (1:1–2:5)

Following Joshua's death, the Israelites inquire of Yahweh: "Who shall go up first for us against the Canaanites?" (1:1). The answer is Judah, followed by a lengthy account of the possession of territory by some tribal groups and the failures of others.

A vignette of Caleb and his daughter, who becomes the wife of Othniel, a future judge, appears in 1:11-15. Caleb epitomizes success in the south, in contrast to failure by the northern tribes. The House of Joseph is successful at Bethel, but the tribes of Manasseh, Ephraim, Zebulon, Asher, Naphtali, and Dan fail to drive out the locals.

In addition to the litany of "could not drive out" statements, there are pointed references to the persistence of the Canaanites in the land. Verses 28 and 33 point out that the Canaanites are put to forced labor after the Israelites grow strong.

In response to the failures of Israel, the angel of Yahweh delivers a message of judgment at Bochim: Yahweh will not drive out all the inhabitants of the land because they have disobeyed Yahweh's command to make no "covenant with the inhabitants of this land" and to "tear down their altars" (2:2). Their gods will be a snare to the tribes.

The Amorites maintain their position and force the Israelite Danites back into the hill country, again with the qualification that the Amorites, like the Canaanites, are made subject to forced labor.

B. Prologue II (2:6-10)

The second prologue consists of a reprise of Joshua's dismissal of the tribes to their own inheritances and a résumé of Joshua's work and death, which is followed by a new generation, one that does not "know the Lord or the work that he had done for Israel" (v. 10).

C. Rationale for the judges (2:11–3:6)

After the death of Joshua (2:7-9), another generation arises that does not recognize what Yahweh has done for the people (2:10). Israel then follows a cycle: (1) disloyalty to Yahweh, the worship of other gods, oppression by their enemies, and the inability to win in battle; (2) intervention from Yahweh through the raising up of judges to deliver the Israelites from the power of their enemies; (3) a relapse of behavior into following other gods. (See also 10:6-16)

God is "moved to pity" by the unrepentant people groaning from oppression (2:18). After continued disobedience, however, an angry Yahweh declares that the nations left by Joshua will not be driven out but left to test Israel's loyalty. This declaration is followed by a list of the nations and the intermarriage of Israelites with them. The conquest is not complete, signifying that the people have not obeyed Yahweh, and that Yahweh has changed plans for Israel and the land, as indicated in the message of the angel in 2:1-5.

II. Accounts of the judges (3:7–16:31)

A. The first seven judges (3:7–10:5)
1. (3:7-11) Othniel, Caleb's younger brother, delivers the Israelites from a king whose name means "Double Trouble."
2. (3:12-20) Ehud of Benjamin, a left-handed man, kills King Eglon of Moab.
3. (3:31) Shamgar, son of Anath, uses an ox goad to kill 600 Philistines.
4. (4:1–5:31) Deborah, from Ephraim, and Barak, from Naphtali, lead a coalition of tribes to victory over Sisera, commander of the army of King Jabin of Hazor.
5. (6:1–9:57) Gideon of Manasseh ends the oppression of the Midianites and fathers Abimelech, who becomes the ruler of Shechem. He is denounced by Jothan, the youngest son of Gideon (Jerubaal).

6. (10:1-2) Tola of Issachar is from the hill country of Ephraim.
7. (10:3-5) Jair of Gilead has 30 towns and 30 sons who ride 30 donkeys.

B. Five additional judges (10:6–16:31)
1. (10:17–12:7)Jephthah of Gilead sacrifices his daughter.
2. (12:8-10) Ibzan of Bethlehem has 30 sons, all of whom marry non-Israelite wives.
3. (12:11-12) Elon of Zebulun.
4. (12:13-15) Abdon of Ephraim has 40 sons and 30 grandsons, riding 70 donkeys.
5. (chs. 13–16) Samson, a Nazirite of Dan who has unbelievable strength, wisdom, and sexual promiscuity, struggles with the Philistines, winning victory in his death.

III. Disintegration of the tribes (chs. 17–22)

A. Micah and his idol and the Levite priest (17:1-13)
B. The Levite and the migration of the tribe of Dan (18:1-31)
C. Rape of the Levite's wife in the tribe of Benjamin (19:1-30)
D. Intertribal war with Benjamin; attack against Jabesh-Gilead; abduction of 200 women of Shiloh (20:1–21:25)

Commentary and Reflection

Perhaps we could call the book of Judges a book of weeping. In the early part the Israelites are depicted as weeping and making sacrifices to Yahweh. At the end of the book they weep again over the intertribal war with the Benjaminites and the unremitting crime at Gibeah. In this struggle, Judah is chosen to go up first, not against the Canaanites (as in 1:1-2), but against fellow Israelites of the tribe of Benjamin. In chapter 10 the Israelites are oppressed by the Philistines and the Ammonites, resulting in their crying out to Yahweh because of their great distress. This account moves on to Jepthah's successful efforts in breaking the oppression of the Ammonites, but ends with his young daughter weeping for her virginity before her death because of her father's foolish vow. Her wails on the mountains are echoed every year during four days of lamentation by the daughters of Israel. The history of Israel is a "trail of tears," especially for women. Jephthah's daughter has many sisters.

In the present book, stories are gathered around twelve leaders who judge Israel for varied periods of time. Othniel, Deborah, and Gideon rule for 40 years. During Ehud's leadership the land has rest for 80 years. Samson judges Israel for 20 years. The shortest judgeship is 6 years assigned to Jephthah, except for Shamgar, who has no time assigned to him. Abimelech, who tries to be a king but who is not counted as a judge, rules Israel for 3 years (9:22). Added together without critical reflection, the years total 410, almost certainly not the intent of the writer. A reasonable estimate of the time span would be about 150 years, the numbers being typical for a generation (20 or 40 years) and the like.

I. The judges

In Hebrew usage the term "judge" means "to govern" or "to rule," but in the book of Judges the word is identified with "deliverer" or "savior." The "saviors," or "liberators," "judged" Israel in the sense of freeing the people from oppression and establishing order and stability among the tribes. For example, Othniel "judged Israel" and delivered them, so "the land had rest forty years" (3:11). In other words, the land was at peace during the time of the judges, enjoying a state of stability.

The judges are frequently referred to as charismatic leaders, gifted by God with power for certain tasks. This is appropriate for leaders said to have been "raised up" by Yahweh and energized by the spirit of Yahweh. How the judges become authoritative leaders is not recorded in most cases, but we have the well-known call account of Gideon (ch. 6) and the drafting of Jephthah by the elders of Gilead (ch. 11), and a special birth, dedication, and blessing in the case of Samson (ch. 13).

Three major types of deliverance are brought about by the judges. These will be discussed in relation to certain leaders and will be followed by a brief consideration of chapters 17–21, which reflect the absence of judges or kings. The types of deliverances are as follows and illustrated by the leaders indicated: freedom from the threat of Canaanite city-states

(Deborah-Barak); deliverance from oppression by peoples on the perimeters of the land (Gideon and Jephthah, from Midianites and Ammonites); and deliverance from the main competitors with the Israelites for the hill country (Shamgar and Samson, from the Philistines).

A. Deborah-Barak and the Canaanite city-states

This story is given in both a prose narrative (ch. 4) and in poetic form known as the Song of Deborah (ch. 5), which is often considered to be one of the oldest parts of the Old Testament.

Deborah is a prophet who judges Israel while sitting under her palm tree in the hill country of Ephraim ("between Ramah and Bethel"). She summons Barak to lead the Israelite warriors. Their Canaanite counterparts are Jabin and Sisera. Sisera may have been the military leader of a coalition of Canaanite groups and Philistines.

Deborah's role in the narrative is ambiguous. The text identifies her as a prophet, with the Israelites coming to her "for judgment." She is deeply involved in the deliverance of Israel from Canaanite oppression, even going to battle with Barak, but when she gives "judgment" for Israel, she gives Yahweh's decision regarding the situation. She is the median of the call of Yahweh to Barak, and her going with him embodies the presence of Yahweh at his side. Her actual military role, if any, is obscure. She is an agent of the real victor—the Divine Warrior, Yahweh, the God of Israel. While Sisera deploys his chariots of iron, Deborah deploys the fighting power of Yahweh, who goes out before Barak. Jabin and Sisera are destroyed, and Yahweh's great force convulses the earth with a flood of water and an earthquake.

Deborah is not the only woman in this story. She tells Barak that the glory of the campaign will not be his, "for the Lord will sell Sisera into the hand of a woman" (4:9). Seemingly, the woman would be Deborah, but rather it is Jael, the wife of Heber the Kenite, who had encamped at a place near Kedesh in the north.

The account is fraught with irony, as Sisera escapes from the destruction of his army and flees to the tent of Jael. He is warmly greeted by her. (The sexual aspects of the narrative are muted, but a latent eroticism is present.) Sisera assumes he is safe in the tent of a cooperative woman who is not an Israelite, and he addresses her as if he were a male who has control: "Stand at the entry of the tent, and if any [man] comes and asks you, 'Is anyone here?' say, 'No' " (4:20). But while Sisera sleeps, Jael drives a tent peg through his temple (or possibly his lips). Barak comes to the tent in pursuit of Sisera. Jael goes out again to meet a man running toward her tent and invites him in to see the man he is seeking, lying with a tent peg driven through his head. How the mighty have fallen—by the hand of a woman!

Thus, two women are the chief human actors in this story of Israel's deliverance. Barak, of course, plays an important and necessary role, but he is "lightning" (the meaning of his name) between Deborah ("bee") and Jael ("she-goat"). Israel's deliverance is effected by a woman prophet and a non-Israelite woman. Deborah is praised as "a mother in Israel" (5:7), and Jael is declared to be the "most blessed of women" (5:24). In contrast, Sisera's mother and her attendants sing praises of war, pillage, and rape while they wait in vain for him to return home. But Sisera made the mistake of going to battle against Yahweh, the divine warrior of Israel, and he paid the price.

B. Gideon and the Midianites

This account is representative of Israel's deliverance by Yahweh from the oppression of foes on the perimeter of the land. In the larger framework, the stories of Othniel, Ehud, and Jephthah would be included. In the case of Gideon, it is the Midianites who terrorize the land with their camels and other livestock, confiscating crops and livestock of the Israelites. As warriors, and later traders, they had an advanced technological culture in the southern region of the Transjordan, and possibly were part of a five-city federation.

Space does not allow for a full summary of the well-known Gideon stories. Two aspects seem worth some comment, however. First, there is a marked character of sign-seeking and test-making about the narratives, as found in chapters 6 and 7. Gideon's resistance to his call—similar in general respects to the calls of Moses, Barak, and Jeremiah—involves him in his famous request for the sign of the fleece, wet and dry. Earlier he had requested a sign from the angel who came to him at the threshing floor, and received it when the angel caused fire to consume the food he brought.

Concern for some sort of testing is woven deeply into the narratives; chance appears at every turn. Gideon's father, Joash, puts the burden of proof for condemning Gideon on Baal: "If he is a god, let him contend for himself, because his altar has been pulled down" (6:31).

Yahweh provides the big test in the story. The fighters assembled with Gideon to fight the Midianites are reduced in number by divine command because they are too many: "Whoever is fearful and trembling, let him return home" (7:3). As a result of the command, 22,000 go home, but 10,000 are left. Yahweh then instructs Gideon to take the troops down to the water, "and I will sift them out for you there" (7:4). The verb "sift" is normally used for smelting of metal or refining, but "testing" is the real meaning.

The procedures of holy war are exemplified in this passage. The reduction of the troops to 300 is a test of faith, so that credit for victory will not be taken away from Yahweh. The test in this case is presented as a grim one. The Midianites are described as having huge forces and resources. The 300 with Gideon hold torches in their left hands and horns to blow in their right; their battle cry is " a sword for the Lord and for Gideon" (7:20). The sword, of course, symbolizes the sword of each Midianite against his fellow fighter, which causes their army to run away in a rout. The quest for signs and tests is indicative of a struggle for faith. God often honors such requests as means toward gaining full trust and obedience.

A second major aspect of the Gideon narratives is the indication of major internal trouble in the life of the people. This is not the first appearance of domestic problems (see the Song of Deborah, ch. 5). In the Gideon narratives we find a major problem with Baal worship, a practice condemned by the narrator's comments in 2:11-14. Chapter 8 tells of Gideon's pursuit of the two kings of the Midianites, Zebah and Zalmunna, east of the Jordan. This material is characterized by discord and violence, emerging from the Ephraimites and the towns of Succoth and Penuel. Gideon personally kills the two kings, after his firstborn son, Jether, refuses to do so. He also punishes the offending towns severely, motivated in part by his desire for vengeance for the deaths of his close kinsmen at Tabor.

The aftermath of Gideon's campaign is especially telling. Gideon refuses kingship and affirms the rule of Yahweh. However, he asks for and receives an enormous amount of booty taken from the Midianites, with an emphasis on a large quantity of gold and silver jewelry, along with fine garments. Gideon makes an ephod (a priestly garment), probably for divination procedures, but possibly as a garment to adorn a statue used in worship of the gods. In any case, the ephod "becomes a snare to Gideon and to his family." There is a failure of loyalty to Yahweh and religious confusion. A note in 8:33 tells us that after Gideon died, the Israelites "prostituted themselves with the Baals, making Baal-berith their god."

The long narrative in chapter 9 contains the account of Abimelech, a son of Gideon, trying to make himself king at Shechem. The story also contains the fable of Jotham (vv. 8-15). Abimelech's short and violent rule as king ends with his death as he tries to capture the town of Thebez. Mortally wounded when a woman throws a millstone on his head, he has his armor-bearer kill him lest people say a woman killed him.

C. Jephthah and the Ammonites

Jephthah is the illegitimate son of Gilead and a prostitute. Forced out of the family/clan realm of life by his half-brothers, Jephthah becomes a powerful warrior, leading raids with a band of outlaws.

The elders of Gilead summon Jephthah home to lead the fight against the Ammonites. Jephthah agrees to do so on the condition that he be installed as the leader of the Gileadites. A long and complex narrative recounts Jephthah's unsuccessful negotiations with the Ammonites and the successful attack that follows. Israel's claim to Transjordan territory is validated by the narrative (11:12-33). The story continues with the fulfillment of a vow made by Jephthah that results in the sacrifice of his daughter, his only child. This is followed by an account of an attack and war with the Ephraimites (12:1-6). Jephthah's victory is marred by warfare among the Israelites, as were the achievements of Gideon.

Jephthah's vow and the sacrifice of his daughter draw most of our attention in the narrative. There seems to be no reason for the vow. Jephthah is empowered by the spirit of Yahweh and thus should need no vow. The text suggests that Jephthah does not trust the gift of the spirit and moves to dependence on his vow. The vow seems like theological overkill, or else it represents the smugness of a warrior who wants to lay an obligation on Yahweh for personal glory through a smashing victory. Note, Jephthah's vow to offer as a burnt-offering "whoever comes out of the doors of my house to meet me" (11:31) could refer to an animal, but it almost certainly means a human being in this text.

Trapped by his vow, Jephthah blames his daughter. Further, he refuses to break his vow. Has she known about the vow? Is it public knowledge? Does she go out knowingly to meet her father?

We miss any willingness on the part of Jephthah or his daughter to struggle with God over this matter. Likewise, there is no indication that Jephthah offers to take the place of his daughter or even to give up the glory of his victory. True, Abraham does not protest the command to sacrifice Isaac, but the context is different. Isaac's binding on the altar was the result of faith, but Jephthah's vow is made on his own initiative and comes out of distrust; it is not a test of faithfulness.

Jephthah's faith is that of a "true believer," one who has a blind obedience that God does not want and one who violates the repeated commandments of Yahweh against child sacrifice. Jepthah is unwilling to take the consequences of his own mistakes and repent of vows he should not have made. He values human life less than the satisfaction of his own convictions and converts faith into an instrument of death, a faith marked by intolerance, absolutism, and legalism. The ugly head of such faith has reared itself too often in Christian history.

Jephthah is included in the list of people of faith in Hebrews 11:32, along with Gideon, Barak, Samson, David, and Samuel. One can hope that this inclusion is based on his willingness to be called into service after being made an outcast as the son of a prostitute. Despite the terrible consequences of his rash vow, he is remembered as one of the successful judges of Israel, who led the people over their Ammonite enemies. Nevertheless, his vow and the sacrifice of his daughter remain forever as testimony against him, and the wails of the daughters of Israel echo through the centuries. Jephthah is a complex character: strong and weak, worthy of admiration and condemnation.

D. Samson and the Philistines

The account of Samson begins with an ominous note for the Israelites: in response to evil done "in the sight of the Lord," the Israelites are allowed to be under Philistine control for forty years. The exact origin of the Philistines is unknown, but they were a part of a larger movement of people known as the Sea Peoples from the Aegean-Asian basin that occurred around 1200 BCE due to socioeconomic problems.

With Egyptian help, the Philistines settled in the coastal area of Palestine, where they gained control of the major towns and organized them into five city-kingdoms: Gaza, Ashkelon, Ashdod, Ekron, and Gath (see Josh 13:2-3; Judg 3:1-3). The Philistines had a technologically advanced culture, leaving behind evidence of the use of iron in weapons and tools, fine pottery, architecture, and the use of chariots and superior tactics in warfare. The Philistines seem to have adopted the local Canaanite religion. Temples to

Dagon (a Semitic god of rain and fertility) at Gaza, Ashdod, Beth-shan, and a temple for the goddess Astarte are present in the biblical stories.

Samson's mission is to "begin to deliver Israel from the hand of the Philistines" (13:5; see 1 Sam 10:5; 13:23–14:16; 2 Sam 23:13-17). Gregory Mobley (*Samson, the Liminal Hero*) labels Samson a "liminal hero," "liminal" being an adjective from the Latin word for "threshold" or "border." Samson shows a liminal character in several instances: when he moves back and forth between the Danites in the low hills and the Philistines in the coastal areas; when he moves between rural and town life, field and house; and when he moves between the people of Yahweh and the people of Dagon, the Philistine god. Even in his home and in his burial, he is liminal. He is identified as "between Zorah and Eshtaol" (13:25; 16:37), living in the open country between the towns, where he is stirred by Yahweh's spirit and where he is buried.

Perhaps it is worthwhile to observe that the entire book of Judges has a liminal character. Noticeable is Deborah's work as a prophet and judge "between Ramah and Bethel" (4:5). Judges covers a period between the settlement led by Joshua and the monarchy led by Samuel, Saul, and David. The judges are also liminal, operating primarily in villages outside the city-states (note the 30 towns/villages of Jair's sons in 10:3). This is also the character of the entire history from Joshua through Kings. Israel is in between promise and exile, between salvation and punishment.

The physical feats of Samson are legendary: He tears a roaring lion apart barehanded. He kills 30 Philistines at Ashkelon and takes away their spoil and garments. Another time he kills 1,000 men with the jawbone of a donkey. He carries away the gate of Gaza to Hebron (some 40 miles). He flings off ropes and thongs binding his arms and hands. He pulls his long hair out of a web woven by Delilah—pin, loom, and web. Finally he brings down the pillars of the temple of Dagon at Gaza onto the lords and people of the Philistines.

Samson was ordained to be a "Nazirite to God" before he was born (13:1). The norms for Nazirites involved: no wine or strong drink, no razor used on the head, no contact with the dead (probably including dead animals), and a special vow dedicating themselves as a "Nazirite to Yahweh."Obviously, Samson does not observe all these stipulations. He handles the carcass of a lion, takes the clothes off the dead bodies of the men killed at Ashkelon, and attends a feast where there is much drinking. However, we should probably not assume that all of the Nazirite vows apply to Samson. The no wine-drinking requirement and no contact with anything unclean applies to his mother (13:4-7, 13-14; 16:7), and only the prohibition of cutting hair with a razor applies to Samson. Probably he should be understood as Nazirite in the sense of belonging to and being dedicated to a category of powerful warriors. Unlike many warriors of Israel's past, or future, Samson fights alone, kills Philistines alone, and destroys their property alone. He is the lion-killer of Israel, who champions the cause of the Israelites with the fearsome power of a Nazirite warrior.

Samson's forays into Philistine life are not entirely those of a wild ass of a man who destroys enemies with any weapons at hand. He also invades Philistia with his sexual prowess. In this regard there are three Philistine women involved. Two are unnamed, but the third is named Delilah.

Chapters 14 and 15 tell of a young woman in Timnah whom Samson sees and desires to be his wife. Accompanied by his parents, he returns to Timnah and arranges for a wedding, evidently on his own despite parental reservations. In the feast before the consummation of his marriage, Samson engages the Philistines present in a riddle contest—another demonstration of power and also an effort to gain financial resources at the expense of the Philistines (30 linen garments and 30 festal garments are at stake). Unable to solve the riddle themselves, the Philistine "young men" (probably meaning "warriors"), force Samson's wife-to-be to sweet-talk and nag the answer out of him. The result of this foray into sex and love on Samson's part results in death: Samson kills 30 men at Ashkelon.

In retaliation for the Timnite's father giving his wife-to-be to another man, Samson catches 300 foxes, ties their tails together, and then puts a torch between each pair of tails. The burning foxes destroy the Philistine grain fields, vineyards, and olive groves. The Philistines then burn the man and his daughter. It is not out of order to note that Samson's later affair with Delilah ends in his own death—and in both cases there is major death for the Philistines. Sex and death are closely linked.

Chapter 16 gives the account of the other two Philistine women in Samson's life. The second woman is a prostitute in Gaza, whom Samson visits. After being with her until midnight, he leaves and is still able to carry away the gate structure of the city. The third woman is Delilah.

Delilah lives in the Valley of Sorek, with nothing said about her family or occupation. Delilah's character is veiled, but she readily agrees to seduce Samson and uncover the reason for his strength when the Philistine lords offer her a large sum of money; each of them will give her 1,100 pieces of silver. We are told explicitly that Samson loves Delilah. In a sense, Delilah does not deceive Samson, since she asks directly for the secret of his strength. Rather, she is deceived three times by Samson, who finally reveals to her his secret and ends the game-playing. Actually, Delilah tells the truth in all her conversations, and Samson plays a deadly game of lies. Her house is a house of death, but no one makes Samson go there or stay there. Does he get what he deserves?

A final glimpse of Samson's sexual power may be reflected in the account of his treatment by the Philistines at Gaza. He is put to grinding grain at the prison mill. He is humiliated by being forced to do the work of women—slave women at that. The force of this approach is found in reducing a warrior to the status of a woman (see 1 Sam 26:15; Isa 19:16; Jer 50:37; 51:30 Nah 3:13; cf. Judg 9:53-54). However, there may be a double understanding in the verb for "grind" and the verbs for "entertain" or "perform" (16:21, 25, 27). Some traditional interpretations understand the "grinding" in 16:21 as a euphemism for sexual intercourse, perhaps having Samson to sire

Philistine offspring who would be strong warriors like himself (was Goliath one of these?). What does Samson do when he "performs" for the Philistines?

There are also theological dimensions to Samson's incursions into Philistine life. Samson is empowered by the spirit of God in his remarkable feats of strength. The narrator tells us that at Samson's birth Yahweh "blessed him." Later the spirit of Yahweh "begins to stir him" (13:25). Three times the spirit of Yahweh is said to have "rushed on" him (14:6, 19; 15:14). Made strong by the divine spirit, Samson is a charismatic champion indeed. The Philistines are not dealing with an ordinary Israelite, but with a Yahweh-endowed "judge"—a champion with savage-like strength.

Also, Samson prays to Yahweh twice: for water at a time of great thirst (15:18-19) and for strength for an "act of revenge" to "pay back the Philistines" for his eyes (16:28). In both cases his prayer is answered. We should also notice that Samson is finally overcome when Yahweh leaves him (16:20). Without the divine endowment, Samson is shorn of his strength and becomes like other human beings, as he knows he will. Israelite readers could hardly have failed to notice that this is a form of a familiar theme in the literature of the Deuteronomistic history: victory belongs to Yahweh; no human strength can avail in the affairs of Israel without the divine presence, and no human power can prevail against it.

II. Absence of judges and kings

The closing section of Judges conveys a picture of disintegration and violence. Israel survives, of course, by the grace of God. No strong leader is named who can unify the tribes by his or her actions, although Phinehas, a priest, plays an important role at a crucial time. This section separates into two divisions: the deterioration of worship (chs. 17–18) and the descent into tribal chaos (chs. 19–21). The first section focuses on a man named Micah, a wealthy Ephraimite from the hill country.

The story begins with his return of 1,100 pieces of silver that he has stolen from his mother. We are not told why he returns the money, but probably he does it to be released from his mother's curse. The curse is released, and she asks for the blessing of Yahweh on her son. Ironically enough, she consecrates the money to Yahweh to make an idol, which requires a payment of only 200 pieces of silver. Apparently she keeps the remainder. Micah himself is into idols and has a shrine of his own and his own priest (one of his sons). The narrator's comment in 17:6 is apropos.

A young Levite from Bethlehem, of the clan of Judah, moves north and finds a job with Micah. He is to be paid 10 pieces of silver per year, clothes, and a "living" (not a bad job!). After installing the Levite in his household, Micah is sure that Yahweh will bless him, because he has his own priest (17:7-13). The reader knows right away that this sorry arrangement will not be a blessing.

The tribe of Dan comes into the picture in chapter 18, looking for new territory in which to live. The Danites had been assigned territory in the south, near the coast, but the Amorites pressed them back into the hill country and into the territory of other tribes. Later they move north, finally to settle near Mount Hermon at a place called Laish, which the Danites name Dan. On the way, they rob Micah of his idol, his terraphin, his ephod —and his priest! The Danites seize Laish and the surrounding territory with brutal force, putting "a quiet and unsuspecting people" to the sword and burning the city (18:7, 27-31). There is no deliverer for the people of Laish.

The migration of the Danites is a miniature version of Israel's entrance into and settlement of the land. They send out spies who bring back a favorable report, establish a place of worship, and easily overcome opposition to their efforts to possess the land. The account is a parody, however. They do it all in their own strength and set up Micah's idol for themselves—after hijacking it from Micah and his money-grubbing priest named Jonathan. The irony in this passage is obvious, especially since Jonathan is identified as a grandson of Moses.

A grandson of Moses, who could have stayed safely at home in Bethlehem (17:7), presiding over worship by a graven image? . . . That is what Israel has come to—at least northern Israel at Dan. A cloud, no larger than a hand, appears on the horizon near the end of this account. The sons of Jonathan remain priests until the Babylonian exile (18:30).

The last section of Judges is concerned with the descent of the tribes into destructive chaos (chs. 19–21). Again, a Levite is a central character in the account. Like Micah, he is from the hill country of Ephraim and has a secondary wife from Bethlehem in Judah. The unnamed concubine deserts her husband and goes back to her father's house at Bethlehem. After a protracted time with her father, the Levite and his servant begin the journey home with her (19:1-9).

At Gibeah, a town of the Benjaminites near Jerusalem, the Levite and his party receive hospitality from a non-Gibeahite. During the night the house is assaulted by the men of the town, demanding sexual intercourse with the Levite. The Levite seizes his concubine and puts her out to the lusting thugs. After a night of wanton rape and abuse, the concubine comes and falls at the door of the house where her husband is staying. Finding her there in the morning, the Levite puts her on his donkey (alive? or dead? the text is ambiguous) and takes her home. There he cuts her body into twelve pieces and sends the pieces throughout the territory of Israel as a call for Israelites to respond to the outrage—the outrage of the Gibeahites of course, not his own.

The response of the tribes is described in chapter 20. Gathering as "one body" before Yahweh at Mizpah, their leaders seek to find out the truth of the case. The Levite lies about the matter, blaming everything on the "lords of Gibeah." The result is a disastrous war against Benjamin by the other tribes, a war generated by lies and brutality. After initial defeat, the Israelites defeat the Benjaminites, slaughtering all of them except for 600 men, who save themselves by fleeing to the wilderness. The story of Cain and Abel is playing out in the tribes of Israel.

A third phase of this sordid affair is found in chapter 21. We learn that the Israelites had taken a vow at Mizpah never to give any of their daughters in marriage to Benjamin. They now have a major problem: all of the Benjaminites are dead except for the 600 men who have escaped to the Rock of Rimmon. With no women of their own, the tribe will be lost—the text assumes that the Benjaminite men will marry only Israelite women—and the reader may be excused for wondering why the loss would be so great. To avoid losing the tribe, two blatantly violent operations are carried out to secure wives for the men of Benjamin.

First, the town of Jabesh-Gilead, which did not participate in the attack against Gibeah, is destroyed, and 400 young women are taken and given to the Benjaminites. But still 200 women short, the young women dancing in the vineyards during "the yearly festival of the Lord" at Shiloh are permitted to be abducted by the Benjaminite men. Seemingly satisfied with their solution, the Israelites leave Mizpah and go home to their tribal allotments, having allowed the Benjaminites to go to theirs.

The account of the response of the tribes to the outrage at Gibeah is hardly less than a caricature. The orderly framework of apostasy, oppression, and deliverance has disappeared. Benjamin is saved as a tribe, but all Israel is degraded and endangered. The mission to possess the land (ch. 1) has degenerated into internecine warfare.

The reader should be aware always that the book of Judges is part of a much larger collection of material that extends from Joshua to the end of 2 Kings. The repeated phrase, "in those days, there was no king in Israel" ties together the material with the statements in 17:6 and 21:25 that "all the people did what was right in their own eyes." This state of affairs prepares the way for kingship. The tribes left to themselves degenerate into violence and chaos.

The only person who functions well in these stories is Phinehas, working as a priest at Bethel. He is said to be the grandson of Aaron and is remembered for his fierce zeal for Yahweh, demonstrated by his actions during the incident at Baal of Peor (Num 25:1-18). Ironically enough, his home is at Gibeah. His devotion to Yahweh accords with the strong emphasis on loyalty to Yahweh in Deuteronomy, for example, in chapter 13. He is a Levitical priest who exemplifies what is so terribly missing in the Levites in Judges 17–20.

Phyllis Trible (*Texts of Terror*) calls attention to the juxtaposition, or comparison, of "the extravagance of violence" against women in chapters 19–21 and the stories of Hannah (which follows immediately in the Hebrew text, 1 Sam 1:1–2:21) and Ruth (which follows Judges in the Greek and English texts). She says that these stories speak "a healing word" to the account in Judges 19–21. Also, while the story in chapters 19–21 speaks about ancient Israel, we recognize our own contemporary society in the violence, vengeance, and the abuse of women by men. Trible (87) comments that women are still treated as was the unnamed woman from Bethlehem: "The story is alive, and all is not well." All is not well with Israel, or with us, but Yahweh's purpose for Israel does not cease.

III. The Israelite family

In the Old Testament the basic social structure of Israel before the monarchy is family based. Family is the "glue" that holds Israel together as a people before the beginning of kingship and the state. The Israelites know themselves as descendants of the family of Jacob and his ancestors. The kinship nature of their life is illustrated by the question the Israelites ask as they consider war against the tribe of Benjamin over the incident at Gibeah (20:23).

In ancient times, tribal kinship could be political as well as by blood. A family or clan could occasionally shift from one tribe to another. Tribes themselves could divide or merge. The nearest equivalent to what we call "family" or "household" is the Hebrew term translated as "father's house," which has been defined as a male-dominated, multigenerational household. The multigenerational aspect appears in the Tenth Commandment, which prohibits coveting a "neighbor's house" and indicates the nature of house as wife, manservant, maidservant, ox, donkey, or "anything that belongs to your neighbor" (Exod 20:17). Thus, family households may include people who are not physically related (in-laws, adoptees, slaves, resident aliens), and genealogies may reflect political alignments as much as or more than direct family relationships.

The multigenerational aspect of family households most likely included the living and the dead. Old Testament texts are not very explicit, but careful analysis leads to the conclusion that family rites included the recall and honor of deceased kin. This facet of family life is reflected in the great concern for family burial sites; for example, in the case of Abraham and his family. The dead kin continued to be members of the household.

The leadership of early Israel appears in Old Testament texts as primarily familial. Authority seems to have been vested in two groups: the elders and the "men of" a town, region, or tribe—that is, the legally-free men able to bear arms and exercise the decisions of war and peace. Before the development of the monarchy, leadership above the family-clan-tribal level seems mostly episodic and limited, as with the "judges" in the book of Judges.

The family-household concept appears prominently in the writings of Joshua–Kings. The reader will readily recall the family narratives of Rahab, Achan, Caleb and his daughter, Gideon, Samson, Micah, the Levite and his concubine, Naomi and Ruth, Samuel and Eli, and especially the families of Saul and David. The family narratives of Joshua–Kings are preceded by the family history of Israel's ancestors in Genesis 12–50. Although the family became less central for Israel's existence during the time of the monarchy and the state, family life continued to be important, and undoubtedly became central again in the exilic and postexilic periods when the monarchy and the state existed no more.

The major characteristics of Israelite family-kinship groups include the following. First, families were closely related to land and for the most part lived in villages or hamlets of 50 to 150 people. Archaeological evidence indicates clusters of houses (mostly of a four-room design) arranged rather haphazardly, although usually in groups forming a rough oval pattern and sometimes with a central open space probably used for keeping village livestock. The villages had no walls or defense systems and likely no public buildings. The communities seem to have been autonomous and made up of self-sufficient family groups.

Second, the households of the villages, which were extended kinship groups, lived in an agricultural economy centered around the production of small grain (wheat and barley), tree and vine crops (olive trees and grapevines), livestock (mostly sheep and goats), and vegetable gardens (herbs, spices, onions, etc.). The evidence of trade outside the villages is limited. The clusters of houses in the villages appear to have shared common courtyard space for cooking and other domestic activities. In brief, these clusters housed extended families, probably composed of a senior, nuclear family surrounded by children and other people forming what Carol Meyers calls "a multi-generational compound family."

Third, family identity was based primarily on kinship and land, which is evident in the book of Ruth. However, religion was also a factor of identity. Family contexts appear as basic, forming a substratum for the people and nation-based worship of Yahweh. But families also had their own gods. Most likely the family gods had personal names. In the present texts Yahweh is the name used, but this can be the result of reinterpretation after Yahwism became the established religion of the state. The ancestral deities were known by a series of other names. Among these names, "El" was prominent, for example, El-Elyon, El-Bethel, and El-Shaddai. "Baal" was also used. However, the worship of Yahweh was undoubtedly part of the family religion of some households, and it became much more important when the monarchy and the temple established Yahwism as the official religion of Israel. The Old Testament indicates major efforts by the official religion to modify and control family worship.

Personal identity was construed fundamentally in communal terms. Family life formed a collectivity, woven around kinship, land, work, and religion. The individual self was merged with the family, with accomplishments viewed collectively. People were located on family land in kinship households; they did not choose their living arrangements. Family and community solidarity was, of course, not completely dominant, as a number of narratives in Joshua–Kings demonstrate. Individuals could act on their own, either to withdraw from the communal consensus or else to change it.

We should allow for variety in the formation of family groups. In this regard, the concept of "patriarchy" should not be understood as complete male dominance. Male-dominated multi-generational families is surely correct as descriptive language, but careful analysis points toward a great deal of interdependence and shared authority in family households. Carol Meyers argues that the expression "father's house" should be understood with reference to "descent reckoning along male lines but not necessarily to male dominance in household functioning." The male dominance appears more evident from without than from within, where there are indications of women in managerial roles (e.g. Prov 31:10-31) and references to the family household as "mother's house" (Gen 24:28; Ruth 1:8; Song of Sol 3:4; 8:2). Public persona and private life are often different.

Fourth, the reader of Joshua–Kings can hardly fail to see a high degree of family dysfunction. The families in the narratives characteristically have problems of all sorts: discord, jealousy, seduction, greed, lust, adultery, incest, rape, and murder. "Family values" are conspicuous by their absence. We find little evidence in biblical narratives of "one big, happy family"— except perhaps for the book of Ruth, which presents an island of loyalty in the midst of disloyalty and abuse. The intrigue and violent struggles of the "motley crew" in Judges is replaced by commitment and nonviolent endeavors for family survival and well-being. However, even Ruth is marked by what has been called "compromised redemption," and the performance of the characters in the book is less than sterling. The monarchy is marked by terrible dysfunction in the royal families, beginning with Saul and David. David's family is plagued by his adultery with Bathsheba, the murder of her husband Uriah, and a lack of discipline, leading to the tragic revolt of Absalom and an intra-family struggle for power leading to the reign of Solomon.

The dysfunctional nature of most biblical families, beginning with Genesis 4, is a striking feature of the realism of the Bible and extends into the New Testament, most notably in the case of Jesus of Nazareth and his family. A process of "refamilization" clearly existed with Jesus and his disciples and in the early churches, as expressed in the words of Jesus in Mark 3:35: "Whoever does God's will is my brother and sister and mother." The limits of family life are reset in terms of the kingdom of God. This "re-familization" process produces tension with the domestic codes for household life found in passages that seek to stabilize family life in the traditional style of households (see Col 3:12-4:6; Eph 5:21-6:9; 1 Pet 2:13-3:7). The very existence of these passages, of course, points to problems in family life. The Christian faith can destabilize *and* stabilize.

The biblical realism reminds us of the fact that healthy family life is one of the most difficult achievements in human affairs. The close relationships and built-in tensions produce powerful forces of disruption, frequently abusive and violent in nature. The outsider may fail to detect that apparent success in family life masks deep fissures under the surface through which disastrous eruptions may boil. In this regard, the modern reader will feel at home with the Bible—too much at home perhaps. On the other hand, the biblical narratives encourage us because God works through the flawed families. This is preeminently true with the case of David's house. Yahweh chooses to carry out the divine purpose through this family racked by violence, adultery, rape, murder, rebellion, and deception—a moral jungle and an unsavory mess. But the grace of God often works through such "earthen vessels," and from this we take hope.

Conclusion

The book of Judges is composed of a kaleidoscope of accounts, loosely strung together to tell the story of Israel's attempt to live in the promised land without a king. Many people are named in the book, and some important ones are without names. Brilliant examples of leadership are found, such as that of Caleb and his daughter Achsah, Othniel, Deborah, and the earlier career of Gideon. The combinations of strength and weakness are striking —none more so than in Samson.

Overall, the book represents a decline from the book of Joshua, "a downward spiral" from faithfulness to sin and inter-nicine war—a downward political and religious spiral. Olson notes three phases in the judge stories: (1) judges who are mostly victorious and faithful (3:7–5:31); (2) a transitional phase beginning a downward slide (6:1–10:5) and reaching a climax in the abortive attempt of Abimelech to make himself king (ch. 9); and (3) further decent into military failure, lack of faith, and personal tragedy (10:6–16:31). These stages are fol-lowed, by the disintegration and violence of a period without any judges recorded (chs. 17–21), when "everyone does what is right in his/her own eyes."

In the discussion of Samson as a "liminal hero"—that is, one who belongs to the border, moving back and forth between this place and that, this group of people and that—it was suggested that the entire book of Judges has a liminal nature, an "in between" book. Deborah sitting as a prophet and judge under a palm tree "between Ramah and Bethel in the hill country of Ephraim" represents this major theme. In fact, all of the judges operate in between the major towns and power centers, in "the hill country," and Jephthah operates as a leader of a band of "worthless fellows" outside of the territory of Gilead in the "land of Tob," well to the east of the Jordan.

Probably, this liminal character of the content of the book of Judges represents the historical reality of the development of the Israelite tribes in Palestine. From about 1400 to 1000 BCE, Palestine was dominated by city-states, Canaanite and Philistine, nominally under the control of Egypt. By about 1200 BCE, the big powers, including Egypt, lost control of the trade routes, and there was a breakdown of the economy in the city-states. Warfare among the states and economic distress led to disorder and unrest in the major settled areas. Settlements in the hill country increased during this period and reflected movement of indigenous settled people to the sparsely populated highlands, augmented by the intrusion of outside groups such as the Israelites. This process led to the growth of tribes with new lifestyles in the "in between" territory around and away from the city-states. Until David took Jerusalem and made it his center of power, no Israelite leader operated out of a major city, except for the disastrous effort of Abimelech to establish himself as a city-state king at Shechem.

Readers of the book of Judges will find plenty of ambiguous people and repulsive deeds. In many respects it is a violent and nasty book, no doubt reflecting the reality of life far from the vision in the book of Joshua of the way the tribes should live. Readers may be tempted to turn away from Judges, but every Christian should know that periods in the history of Christianity have been every bit as aborrent as Judges.

The book is not bereft of all hope, however. Bound with bronze chains and blinded by the Phillistines, Samson's hair begins to grow again, and Shiloh remains as a center of Yahweh worship while an idol sanctuary operates at Dan. God is active throughout the book; the divine purpose of redemption through a chosen people in a promised land is never rejected. The tribes fail, but Yahweh does not; the book asks for a new future. The message of this book is that of the faithful grace of God.

For Further Reading

Auld, A. Graeme, *Joshua, Judges, and Ruth.* The Daily Study Bible Series. Philadelphia: Westminster, 1984.

Dunston, Robert C. "Judges." *Mercer Commentary on the Bible.* Edited by Watson E. Mills, et al., 243-57. Macon GA: Mercer University Press, 1995.

Fewell, Dana Nolan. "Judges." *The Women's Bible Commentary.* Edited by Carol A. Newsom and Sharon H. Ringe, 67-77. Louisville KY: Westminster/John Knox, 1992.

Gunn, David M. "Joshua and Judges." *The Literary Guide to the Bible.* Edited by Robert Alter and Frank Kermode, 102-21. Cambridge MA: Belknap Press, 1987.

Mayes, A. D. H. *Judges.* Old Testament Study Guides. Sheffield: JSOT Press, 1985.

Meyers, Carol. "The Family in Early Israel." *Families in Ancient Israel.* Edited by Leo G. Perdue. Louisville KY: Westminster/John Knox, 1997.

O'Connor, M. "Judges." *The New Jerome Commentary.* Edited by Raymond E. Brown, Joseph A. Fitzmyer, and Roland E. Murphy, 132-44. Englewood Cliffs NJ: Prentice Hall, 1990.

Olson, Dennis T. "The Book of Judges." *The New Interpreter's Bible.* Edited by Leander E. Keck, et. al., 723-888. Volume 2. Nashville: Abingdon, 1998.

Yee, Gale A., ed. *Judges and Method: New Approaches in Biblical Studies.* Minneapolis: Fortress, 1995.

Ruth

Why is the book of Ruth read at the Jewish festival commemorating the giving of the law at Sinai? Because in it we see an exemplary figure—Ruth—who does the will of God, even though she is a Moabite. Her fidelity to God's law and commandments is a model worthy of imitation by all Israelites and others. Whereas Joshua–Kings shows the people going from living in the promised land to living in exile, Ruth offers a glimpse at what life could be like if lived in accordance with Yahweh's will. Living in the land requires fidelity, commitment, and endurance. It requires that one love God and each other with heart, mind, and soul.

In Christian Bibles, Ruth is placed after the book of Judges, following the arrangement of the Greek and Latin texts. Ruth 1:1 sets the story in "the days when the judges ruled," although the famine referred to in this verse is not mentioned in Judges. In this position, between Judges and 1 Samuel, Ruth slows the flow of the narrative at the end of Judges and prepares for the monarchy in Samuel–Kings. The last word in the book of Ruth is the name "David," a great-grandson of Ruth, and the first appearance of the name in the Bible. The central theme of Joshua–Kings also appears since the book deals with land, exile, and return.

In the Hebrew Bible, the book of Ruth is found between Proverbs and the Song of Songs. In Jewish tradition, it belongs to the five scrolls read at the main festivals of the Jewish ecclesiastical year—the other four being Song of Songs, Lamentations,

Ecclesiastes, and Esther. The position in the Hebrew Bible is an understandable one, since Ruth follows immediately after the tribute to the worthy woman of power in Proverbs 31:10-31 and immediately before the Song of Songs, which sets forth a stirring tribute to love by a woman and her lover.

It is interesting to consider the contrast between Naomi and the unnamed woman in Judges 19 who leaves her husband and returns to her family in Bethlehem with terrible consequences. More relevant perhaps is the contrast between Delilah, a non-Israelite woman who uses the sexual love of Samson to result in his death, and Ruth, who uses sex to bring forth life. Samson and Boaz are both described as strong men, although different words are used (see Judg 16:5; Ruth 2:1). Looking ahead to Hannah, the barren wife in 1 Samuel 1, we note that the birth of a child to Ruth and to Hannah is described as the "giving" of Yahweh (see Ruth 4:13; 1 Sam 1:11, 27). In intertextual terms, Ruth belongs to a series of biblical stories of women who triumph over infertility, usually by unconventional means: Sarah, Lot's daughters, Rebekah, Rachel, and especially Tamar (Gen 38).

Ruth 1:1 suggests an early date for the writing of the book, but its position among the Writings in the Hebrew canon suggests a later date, probably from the exilic or postexilic periods. Because of the literary nature of the book, commentators vary widely in their conclusions regarding date. The story is plausible, but probably not intended to be read as a strictly historical account. It is a short story, a literary creation that many would probably call fiction. The basic story itself may be quite old, going back to premonarchical times, but the present book comes later. Fortunately, the message of the book does not depend upon the date when it was written. Like parables, it is representative and timeless.

Outline

I. Bethlehem to Moab to Bethlehem (1:1-22)

A. Prologue (1:1-7)

Elimelech, his wife Naomi, and their sons Mahlon and Chilion move from Bethlehem in Judah to Moab because of famine in their home territory. They are Ephrathites, a

RUTH

clan group in Judah encompassing Bethlehem and also linked to David. The bittersweet nature of the story that follows is signaled by the names: Elimelich = "the King (Yahweh) is my God," Naomi = "Winsome" or "My Delight," Mahlon and Chilion = "Sick and Dying."

An important feature of the story is the long tradition of antipathy between Israel and Moab. The beginning of Moab is traced back to the sexual intercourse between Lot and his two daughters (Gen 19:30-38). The incident at Baal of Peor (Num 25:1-4) is linked to the "daughters of Moab" who invited the people to make sacrifices to their gods, which resulted in Israel's being "yoked" to the god Baal. The Moabites are banned from the assembly of Yahweh because they did not provide food for the Israelites during their exodus from Egypt (Deut 23:2-4). A Moabite king hired Balaam to curse Israel (Num 22–24).

After some time Elimelech dies in Moab, leaving Naomi as a widow with two sons. Later the two sons marry Moabite women, Ruth and Orpah, and they live there for about ten years. Then the two sons die, leaving Naomi, Ruth, and Orpah as widows. Hearing that Yahweh has "considered his people and given them food" (v. 6), Naomi sets out with her two daughters-in-law to return to the land of Judah. Up to this point there has been no dialogue in the account, but from now on the story moves by means of conversation between the characters.

B. Dialogue and decisions on the trip (1:8-18)

Naomi's discussion with her daughters-in-law reveals much about her character and her view of life. She urges them to return to their own homes, with a prayer that Yahweh will deal with them in terms of loyal-love and the gift of a secure life in the household of a husband; she assumes they will remarry. Naomi is so conditioned by the customs of patriarchal society that she concludes she has nothing to offer if she has no men to give to her daughters-in-law.

When Naomi appeals to Orpah and Ruth to return home, she discloses her bitterness. She is too old to remarry and have sons, a condition she judges to be worse than that of her daughters-in-law, and one she attributes to "the hand of the Lord" turned against her. Orpah kisses her mother-in-law and goes back, but Ruth clings to Naomi, refusing to leave, refusing to accept the conclusion that women are nothing without men.

Ruth declares in her famous speech of commitment (vv. 16-17) her intention to go with Naomi wherever she may go, to share her living conditions, and to make Naomi's people her people and Naomi's God her God. This is to be a lifelong relationship, for wherever Naomi dies and is buried, Ruth asserts that she will die there and be buried with her. Hers is a love that is stronger than death. She concludes her speech with an oath, which places her in binding loyalty to her mother-in-law: "May the Lord do thus and so to me, and more as well, if even death parts me from you!" (v. 17). Ruth's commitment to Naomi puts her in the class of Abraham and Rebekah, both of whom left their homeland to venture on risky journeys into foreign territory, with no assurance of a welcome and little to be gained. Ruth's strength lies in her loyal love for Naomi.

When Naomi realizes Ruth is determined to go with her, she says nothing more. Why? Perhaps she concludes that there is nothing more to say and that it is time to get on with the journey and her dismal future. Perhaps her silence expresses a degree of resentment and unease, because she had really hoped that both daughters-in-law would stay in Moab so she could put the pain of the land behind her for good. In any case, Moab will go to Bethlehem with Naomi in the person of Ruth the Moabite.

C. Arrival at Bethlehem (1:19-22)

The arrival of Naomi and Ruth stirs the townspeople. "Is this Naomi?" they ask. It is indeed, but she wants no more of the name Naomi. "Call me no longer Naomi (Winsome/ Pleasant); call me Mara (Bitter)." She laments that while she left "full"—the irony of having left in the emptiness and hunger of famine is obvious—Yahweh has brought her back "empty" and bitter. Of course, she had left Bethlehem with a family, which matters more than a famine, so perhaps she can say she was "full" when she left. In any case, Ruth is ignored.

Is Naomi embarrassed about Ruth or fearful of the consequences of having a Moabite daughter-in-law? Repeatedly Naomi blames her condition on God, referring three times to her bitterness and to God as responsible for her woe. Verse 22 provides a transition to emphasis on the return to Bethlehem at the beginning of the barley harvest. The harvest gives promise of new life.

II. Gleaning in the field of Boaz (2:1-23)

A. Narrator's note (2:1)

Boaz is introduced, and now Naomi is not as "empty" as she thinks! Boaz is a "prominent rich man" and a relative of Elimelech. He may be a source of help.

B. Ruth in the field of Boaz (2:2-16)

The initiative in dialogue is now taken by Ruth, who proposes to go to the "the field and glean . . . behind someone in whose sight I may find favor." There is some ambiguity in this statement. "The field" should probably be understood as a reference to all the cultivated land around a town (the same word refers to Moab in 1:1). Is "some-one" just any harvester who will let her glean? Perhaps, but there is an implicit suggestion that she may find some-one who can help her and Naomi. After all, Naomi and Ruth must know that there are family members in the neighborhood, one of whom is probably using the land left by Elimelech. We are not told in the book who is using the land, but possibly it is Boaz or the nearer-kinsman (ch. 4).

One also gets the impression that Ruth does not want to glean grain only around the edges of the fields. She wants to gather grain among the sheaves left by the reapers, a much more productive activity. Her request (v. 7) seems more in keeping with the gleaning stipulations in Deutero-nomy (23:24-25; 24:19-21) than with those in Leviticus. The laws in Deuteronomy are designed to protect the right of access to grain and other crops for the needy and also to protect the farmer from exploitation of this right. Thus, it is appropriate for Ruth to wait for permission to glean among the piles of grain in the main part of the field. She has a marked degree of boldness and persistence, which is no great surprise.

According to verse 3, Ruth "happened" to glean in Boaz's part of the cultivated fields. Is it by chance that she comes to Boaz's harvest, or is it the hidden providence of God? Does Ruth know that this portion of the field belongs to Boaz? Does she head directly for it? Does she make her own good luck? We have no certain answer, but it is hardly by chance. The hidden providence of God is at work.

When Boaz arrives, Ruth is still standing and waiting for a decision from the foreman. Boaz allows Ruth the privilege she has requested. The young men in the harvest are instructed that she is not to be harassed while she gleans among the standing sheaves. Ruth had set out to "find favor" in someone's eyes. The "someone" turns out to be Boaz, who is a member of Naomi's family and can act as a redeemer—as Naomi informs Ruth in verse 20.

Boaz begins to act as a redeemer when he instructs the harvesters to pull out handfuls from the bundles and leave them for Ruth. He also gives her a place among the reapers at mealtime, provides her with food and water, and pronounces a blessing upon her from "the God of Israel, under whose wings you have come for refuge" (v. 12). He commends her highly for her willingness to leave her father and mother and native land and come to a people she does not know, and for what she has done for Naomi.

In turn, Ruth gives herself a status in the larger familial group of Naomi by saying, "You have comforted me and spoken kindly to your servant, even though I am not one of your servants" (v. 13). Perhaps the "not" in the last clause should be read as emphatic, and the statement read as: "and I, I have become as one of your servants!" In any case, the word for "servant" refers to a female servant who is attached to a household, although the *shiphah* (servant) category seems to have been a lowly one, responsible for menial work and probably not normally as eligible for the married status of a concubine (secondary wife) as were the

amah servants. Thus, Ruth expresses her gratitude to Boaz
and implicitly puts a claim on him as her master.

Boaz also shows concern for the safety of Ruth. It is a
risky venture for a foreign young woman to go out in the
fields at harvest time. The fields of Moab may be fields of
death, but the fields of Bethlehem have their danger, too.
Four different verbs are used to refer to the possible threats
to Ruth: touch or molest, hassle, threaten, attack or abuse.
She might not be permitted to glean, or she could be so hin-
dered by the trashy talk and tricks of the reapers that she
would be able to get very little grain. She would also be vul-
nerable to sexual harassment or even sexual assault and
possibly rape.

Thus, Boaz will not allow her to leave his field, even to
get water. He keeps her under his care all day. The young
men are ordered not to "bother" Ruth (but the verb may
mean "not to molest her"), and she is told to stay with the
young women working in the harvest. By verse 16, the
reader knows that Boaz is attracted to Ruth, and a
courtship is underway—between a prominent man of
Bethlehem and a Moabite widow. Will there be a marriage?

C. Ruth as the breadwinner (2:17-23)

Ruth's gleaning venture is very successful, and she goes
back to Naomi at evening time with "an ephah of barley"
(about 30 pounds), along with food left over from her
lunch. In response to the urgent questioning of Naomi,
Ruth tells the story of her day, waiting to the very end of
the account to reveal the name of the man with whom she
worked. Naomi is pleased and identifies Boaz as "one of
our nearest kin (literally, "one of our redeemers"), a potential source of help for them both. Notice that Naomi says
"our"—Ruth is included in the family. In chapter 1 Ruth
clings to a future with Naomi. Now Naomi links her own
future to Ruth and to the enduring love of Yahweh that
does not forsake the living or the dead.

Ruth is counseled to stay with the young women in the
field of Boaz and not to go to another field. This Ruth does
until the end of the harvests (barley and wheat), probably

about seven weeks. Ruth continues living (literally "sitting") with her mother-in-law until the end of the harvests. Will she stay there? Is there another person with whom she will "sit"? Now that harvest time is over, has Boaz disappeared from the story? The narrative pauses, but the reader is not yet satisfied—nor is Naomi.

III. Ruth and Boaz meeting on the threshing floor (3:1-18)

A. Naomi's instructions (3:1-5)

Naomi devises a plan for Ruth, the target of which is Boaz. Naomi assumes that he will eat and drink heavily during the celebration in the fields at the end of harvest. Ruth is told to prepare herself for lovemaking, to move stealthily to the place where Boaz falls asleep, and to lie with him in a sexually provocative way. Naomi is probably gambling on the goodwill of Boaz when she says, "He will tell you what to do." However, she is also gambling with Ruth's well-being when she puts her at sexual and social risk, and with Boaz's standing in the community. Exactly what she wants to happen is not clear.

The narrative suggests that Naomi's goal is to trap Boaz into having sexual intercourse with Ruth, so that a marriage will be necessary, either from the act itself or from a resulting pregnancy. She knows that Ruth is a foreigner, a Moabite woman, whom Boaz would be reluctant to marry because of the risk it would pose to his social standing in Bethlehem. Besides, he has had an entire harvest season to move toward marriage with Ruth without doing so. Naomi and Ruth gamble on a good outcome, but without a man like Boaz, the two women have poor prospects for the future. So they have little to lose; the risk is worth taking.

B. Ruth's mission to the threshing floor (3:6-13)

Ruth carries out her seductive mission, and at midnight Boaz wakes startled (perhaps "shocked") to find a woman he does not know "lying at his feet." Ruth identifies herself by name with the addition of "your servant" (*amah*, not the *shiphah* of 2:13, probably indicating a more

family-oriented relationship and eligibility for marriage).
Ruth then boldly asks for a sexual-marriage relationship
with Boaz as a redeemer: "Spread your cloak (or wing)
over your servant" (v. 9). The erotic nature and the double-
entendres in the narrative are clear: the terms "stealthily,"
"legs/feet" (which can refer to genitals), "uncover/cover,"
"lie down/sleep with," and "know" are all sexual euphe-
misms. In addition, Boaz's speeches in chapter 2 have
sexual overtones with references to eating, drinking, and
so on. The exact nature of the sexual activity of Ruth and
Boaz is not explicitly described, however. The soft curtain
of the midnight darkness drops over the scene, and the
reader is not informed about the physical details—and
properly so.

Boaz's reply is a gracious one, praising Ruth's loyalty
and declaring that she has demonstrated her loyal-love in
not going after "young men, whether poor or rich" (v. 10).
Perhaps her former "loyalty" refers to her loyalty to
Naomi, but there can be little doubt that the loyalty she is
showing now is her willingness to become the lover/wife of
Boaz. This text strongly suggests that Boaz is older, older at
least than the "young men." Ruth's overtly sexual behavior
comes to him as a blessing. Note, we are told nothing about
Boaz's previous marital status, but it seems reasonable to
assume he is unmarried or a widower.

Boaz's response to Ruth, however, should not be read
only in terms of his pleasure in Ruth's sexual willingness
for him rather than for some other man. Ruth's sexual
advances are worthy of his praise, but they bring into play
larger concerns. Ruth's use of the word "cloak/wing"
recalls Boaz's reference to Ruth as having taken refuge
under the "wing/cloak" of Yahweh (2:12). He is aware of
the social and economic situation of Ruth and Naomi,
although there is no discussion of it between Ruth and
Boaz. He is focused on Ruth, but he acknowledges his role
as a "near kinsman"; that is, he has family responsibility
that will not allow him to sexually exploit Ruth. He now
declares her to have the status of a "worthy woman" in the
community (literally, "a woman of strength/power" [Prov
31:10]), and "all the assembly"—the community meeting

place—knows this. In the judgment of Boaz, Ruth is now a part of the family and the community. (In chapter 3 she is not referred to as a Moabite or a foreigner.)

Boaz is now prepared to act as a redeemer for Ruth, but he has a problem: there is a potential redeemer who is nearer kin than he. He must allow this man the opportunity to redeem, if he desires to do so. If he will not, however, Boaz declares on oath: "I will act as next-of-kin for you." Boaz puts aside whatever reservations he may have had about Ruth as a foreigner, or about his own limitations as an older man versus the young men, or about the risks to compromising his social and economic standing at Bethlehem. The combination of sex, loyalty, and redeemer responsibility is a potent one indeed.

C. The morning scene with Naomi (3:14-18)

In accord with Boaz's directive to "lie down until the morning" (v. 13), Ruth lies at his feet until the early dawn, when she leaves under cover of darkness so that it will not be known in the town that "the woman came to the threshing floor" (the Hebrew article here can be read as meaning "a woman"—some particular woman—but I suspect it indicates Ruth was "the woman" to watch and talk about in Bethlehem), a further directive of Boaz, protecting her and himself. Possibly Boaz does not want the nearer-kinsman to know of his meeting with Ruth, so that an element of surprise in the gate can be gained. He fills her "cloak" with "six measures of barley" (an uncertain amount, but probably more than the ephah in 2:17) and then goes to the town.

Ruth returns to Naomi, with her six measures of barley, supposedly to Bethlehem also (by a different route than that of Boaz? Or, perhaps, behind him?). Her report to Naomi has often bothered commentators. She quotes Boaz as saying, "Do not go back to your mother-in-law empty-handed," whereas the conversation in verses 9-15 reports no such thing. In these verses Boaz's attention is focused on Ruth. (Ruth also tells Naomi nothing about her actions at the threshing floor.) Perhaps Ruth tells Naomi what she thinks Naomi wants or needs to hear, or code language is used in these explicit matters. Naomi would have heard the directive "do not go back empty-handed" in a positive way—"empty-handed" is the same word she uses for herself in 1:21. Also when Boaz pledges himself to Ruth, Naomi is implicitly involved; she and Naomi cannot be separated in such family affairs. Again, Ruth does not need to supply Naomi with the details of her tryst with Boaz; it is enough that she was treated well. Thus, Naomi counsels patience to see how the matter will turn out, relying on the persistent nature of Boaz.

IV. Scene at the gate and its sequel (4:1-22)

A. Showdown with the nearer-kinsman (4:1-6)

The reader may ask why Boaz wants to take the risk of a public encounter in the town gate, rather than going privately to the nearer-kinsman and working out a deal. Surely he needs social approval of a marriage to Ruth, who is again referred to as "Ruth the Moabite" (v. 5). As a leader of the community, Boaz needs to make a dubious affair with Ruth into a public affirmation that will protect them both. He acts so that his position in the town ends up strengthened, making virtue out of necessity. This seems to be confirmed by the fact that Boaz's talk in chapter 4 is that of land, name, and family. The talk is male-oriented and quite different from his conversation with Ruth at the threshing floor.

A surprise element appears in verse 3. Naomi owns a piece of land and wants to sell it. Why has she not done this sooner? Has she been saving it as an ace up her sleeve in case the efforts of Ruth failed? Has she wanted to make sure it does not become Ruth's property? Is it being used by some kinsman-redeemer, possibly the nearer-kinsman or Boaz? The text does not tell us, but Boaz seems to play the trump card. The property is probably small and poor in quality, almost worthless economically, but having powerful symbolic value in family and community relationships. It is worth little for agriculture, but enough that Boaz can and does use the property to force the hand of the nearer-kinsman. Naomi knows her man (see 3:18). The reader must be struck by the shrewdness of all three major characters in this book.

The nearer-kinsman is about to pass through the gate when he is called aside by Boaz. A hearing is arranged before ten elders. Boaz puts before them the case regarding Naomi's parcel of land. The nearer-kinsman responds with willingness to act as a redeemer in regard to it. When Boaz says that the redeeming process involves "Ruth the Moabite," however, the nearer-kinsman declines and gives his permission for Boaz to redeem.

The usual interpretation assumes the nearer-kinsman declines the responsibility of redemption because it would involve a marriage to Ruth, a foreign woman. Since Ruth is young enough to bear children, a child by her would inherit the property, plus the expense of the care and feeding of Naomi, Ruth, and any children she might bear. His refusal may be understood in terms of "I cannot afford it"—the risk is too great.

However, verse 5 may be interpreted two ways. The consonantal Hebrew text reads, "on the day you acquire the field from Naomi . . . It will acquire Ruth the Moabite," rather than the marginal reading: "on the day you acquire the field from Naomi you are also acquiring Ruth the Moabite." The consonantal text seems better because the main point is that Boaz intends to marry Ruth and act as her redeemer, regardless of who gets Naomi's field. Of course, any son born to Boaz and Ruth would be the potential heir of the land. Either way the nearer-kinsman stands to lose.

The nearer-kinsman wisely yields to Boaz and declares his intention not to redeem. Remember, neither one has an obligation to marry Ruth, who is not an Israelite. Only Naomi is directly involved, and she is too old to bear a child who could lay claim to the land. Boaz's intention "to maintain the dead man's name on his inheritance" by marrying Ruth deprives the nearer-kinsman of ultimate claim to the land and leaves him responsible for Naomi.

B. The ceremony (4:7-12)

The ceremony of redemption involves the nearer-kinsman taking off his sandal and saying to Boaz: "Acquire it [the land] for yourself" (v. 8). The elders and the people are appealed to as witnesses, and they pronounce a blessing upon Boaz and Ruth.

In some respects this ceremony is like that of the brother in Deuteronomy 25:5-10. There, the brother refuses the responsibility of levirate marriage, which stipulates that if a man dies without a son to be his heir, his brother is to marry the widow in order to have a son who can continue the family heritage of name and land. This text describes the actions that can be taken by the widow and the elders of a town in response to a disobedient brother. The common elements between this passage and the account in Ruth 4 are obvious: widow without heir, location of the ceremony in the gate of the town, the elders acting as a court, the taking off of a sandal from the unwilling man's foot. Several features do not fit the Ruth text, however.

Neither Boaz nor the nearer-kinsman are brothers, so they are not obligated to marry Ruth. There is no threat to spit in the face of the unwilling kinsman. And the sandal is not pulled off the kinsman's foot by a woman. Putting on the sandal is a euphemism for sexual relations. Boaz is determined to "put on the sandal" of marriage with Ruth, leaving the nearer-kinsman little option but to "take off the sandal" of property rights.

The ceremony concludes with the blessing of Boaz (and of Ruth, who is called "this young woman") by the elders and the people at the gate to have children and gain a prominent name in Bethlehem, and that his "house be like the house of Perez, whom Tamar bore to Judah" (v. 12). Yahweh is asked to bless Ruth ("the woman who is coming into your house") so that she may do what it took two matriarchs—Rachel and Leah—to do.

C. The sequel (4:13-22)

Ruth enters the picture again as Boaz "takes her" (to his house?) and she becomes his wife; she is no longer only the Moabite daughter-in-law of Naomi. Suddenly Yahweh appears in the narrative and gives Ruth conception as a result of her intercourse with Boaz. She bears a son, a new son for Naomi, a son through whom the dead will live. Ruth then fades out of the picture.

Now the women of Bethlehem, who greeted Naomi on her return from Moab, bless her, saying, "A son has been born to Naomi." The role of Ruth is affirmed as "your daughter-in-law who loves you," and who is declared to be better than "seven sons to you" (v. 15). But it is Naomi who "takes" the child and becomes his nurse. Ruth has given Naomi grain, but Naomi does not wait for Ruth to give the child to her.

Although parents usually name a child, the women of the neighborhood name the child Obed, meaning "one who serves/worships," perhaps a shortened form of "worshiper of Yahweh." Perhaps we can say that Ruth's final deed for her mother-in-law is to step out of the way and allow Naomi to have center stage. But is Ruth removed from the text in order to guard the child (and David) from the stigma of a Moabite mother? The reader is left to ponder this in his or her heart.

The book of Ruth closes with a short genealogy that leads to David. Two or three things about this list are worthy of attention. First, Mahlon, the husband of Ruth who died in Moab, is not mentioned, even though Boaz has declared that his purpose in marrying Ruth is to maintain his name on his inheritance and in the gate of "his native place" (4:10). The fact that the genealogy is ten genera-tions long (five between Salmon and David) suggests this is not an exact historical account but one tailored to fit a ten-member scenario. Has the name of Mahlon been "blotted out of Israel" because of his Moabite wife?

Second, the genealogy starts with the "descendants of Perez," who is mentioned in the blessing of Boaz. Perez was the son born to Judah by his daughter-in-law, Tamar

(Gen 38). These two stories of non-Israelite daughters-in-law who became mothers of Israel (and of David in particular) are linked together. They were both bold and determined women who used their sexuality in dangerous ways to force men out of their evasive ways and into the assumption of their proper responsibilities. The Canaanite Tamar and the Moabite Ruth subverted conventions and social systems and broke out of their male-imposed repressions. They were both "women of power" who were worthy to have their "works praise them in the city gates" (Prov 31:10, 31). They also join Rahab, the wife of Uriah (Bathsheba), and Mary in the genealogy of Jesus in Matthew 1:2-16.

Conclusion

The book of Ruth cannot be reduced to one simple meaning. The numerous gaps in the story invite the reader to ponder the narrative and its meanings. The book is concerned with basic human situations: famine, the forced move of a family to an alien context, adaptation, death, return to the home place, survival (economic and family), sex, inclusion of an outsider in a community prone to prejudice and exclusion, loyalty, and the often hidden providence of God. Of course, the book focuses attention on the ability of two women to overcome the cruel circumstances of their lives. It portrays faithfulness that works its way through flawed human character and difficult social issues. The book invites us to seek religious truth on a wider scale than in a narrow reading of law and custom. It opens a door to the risky ventures of loyalty, faith, and love that is "as strong as death."

Fewell and Gunn (106) argue persuasively for the "compromising redemption" of the book; a book of both light and shadows, with characters whose motives are less than pure, and with the providence of God largely hidden in the human and communal process. However, their final judgment is that "God is here in this text," in the midst of "mixed motives, somewhere in the complicated relationships, somewhere in the struggle for survival, anywhere there is redemption, however compromised." With eyes to see and ears to hear, the reader will recognize his or her own mixed motives and be thankful for redemption that transcends compromises. The reader will also recognize that the book of Ruth provides a family history that connects the ancestors of Israel with David and the monarchy. The continuity of Israel is found in the continuity of families, and Naomi and Ruth bridge the movement of Yahweh's saving work from family to nation. Israel, the people of God, lives through Ruth and the redemptive faithfulness of God.

For Further Reading

Bush, Frederic W. *Ruth, Esther*. Word Biblical Commentary. Dallas: Word, 1996.

Campbell, Jr., Edward F. *Ruth*. The Anchor Bible. Garden City NJ: Doubleday, 1975.

Farmer, Kathleen A. Robertson. "The Book of Ruth." *The New Interpreter's Bible*. Edited by Leander E. Keck, 891-946. Volume 2. Nashville: Abingdon, 1998.

Fewell, Donna Nolan and David Miller Gunn. *Compromising Redemption: Relating Characters in the Book of Ruth*. Literary Currents in Biblical Interpretation. Louisville KY: Westminster John Knox Press, 1990.

Hamlin, E. John. *Ruth: Surely There Is a Future*. International Theological Commentary. Grand Rapids: Wm. B. Eerdmans, 1996.

Hubbard, Jr., Robert L. *The Book of Ruth*. The New International Commentary on the Old Testament. Grand Rapids: Wm. B. Eerdmans, 1988.

Laffey, Alice L. "Ruth." *The New Jerome Commentary*. Edited by Raymond E. Brown, Joseph A. Fitzmyer, and Roland E. Murphy, 553-57. Englewood Cliffs NJ: Prentice Hall, 1990.

Levine, Amy-Jill. "Ruth." *The Women's Bible Commentary*. Edited by Carol A. Newsom and Sharon H. Ringe, 78-84. Louisville KY: Westminster/John Knox, 1992.

Nielsen, Kirsten. *Ruth: A Commentary*. The Old Testament Library. Louisville KY: Westminster/John Knox Press, 1997.

West, Mona. "Ruth." *Mercer Commentary on the Bible*. Edited by Watson E. Mills, et al., 259-67. Macon GA: Mercer University Press, 1990.

Samuel–Kings

The literature known as Samuel–Kings focuses on the history of Israel under the monarchy, whereas Joshua–Judges, focuses on the history of Israel without kings. Even though there are no actual divisions within Samuel or Kings, in the Bible as we know it, the story progresses as follows:

- 1 Samuel moves to the end of the reign of Saul and the preparation for David to be king.
- 2 Samuel is devoted to the reign of David.
- 1 Kings deals with the end of David's reign, the following reign of Solomon, and the division of the kingdom into the north and south. Beginning in chapter 17, the work of the prophets is emphasized.
- 2 Kings continues the story of the monarchies, leading to the fall of Israel and later Judah into exile. The division into four books is the result of tradition and convenience; the narrative has no major breaks.

Outline

I. The advent of kingship in Israel (1 Sam 1:1–2 Sam 1:27)

A. Samuel's birth; choice as a prophet (1 Sam 1:1–4:1a)

Following his birth to Hannah and Elkanah, Samuel lives at Shiloh with his mentor, the priest Eli. Eli's sons, Hophni and Phinehas, are priests, although they fail in their service to Yahweh. They are condemned in a message from

God to Eli. Samuel is chosen by God to be the prophetic leader of Israel, alongside the priest/king-like leader Eli.

B. The ark of the covenant and the Philistines (1 Sam 4:1b–7:2); Samuel's judgeship (1 Sam 7:3-17)

The Philistines are Israel's most potent competitor for control of the land. They continue as a major military and economic threat until they are overcome by David.

Samuel is established as Israel's leader. The key emphasis in 7:3-17 is repentance. The Deuteronomistic pattern found in Judges is operative here: sin, punishment, repentance, deliverance. Samuel appears here as the last of the judge-deliverers of Israel, and the Israelites enjoy a time of peace and justice.

C. Samuel and the advent of monarchy (1 Sam 8:1–12:25)

The Israelites demand a king so that they "may be like the other nations." Samuel disapproves of the request, but he is overruled by Yahweh because of concern for the suffering of the people (9:15-16; 10:1). Samuel is told to warn the people of the dangers of kingship, which he does at great length (8:10-19; 12:1-25). With the rise of the monarchy in Israel, God raises not judges, but prophets for the people, to speak God's word to the king and the Israelites.

D. Saul's struggle with the Philistines; rejection as king (1 Sam 13:1–15:35)

Saul's first rejection as king occurs in the context of his struggle with the Philistines. The failure of Samuel to follow his own instruction (10:8; 13:8) leaves Saul in a situation of such distress and danger that he makes his own sacrifice (13:8-14). Nevertheless, he is harshly condemned by Samuel, who is not rebuked by the narrator. Saul's second rejection follows his victory over the Amalekites (15:1-35). Because he does not completely follow the mandate of the ban—sparing Agag, the king, and the best livestock—Samuel declares that Yahweh has repudiated him as king and will give the kingship to "a neighbor of yours, who is better than you" (15:28). These texts reflect a power struggle between samuel and Saul—and Saul loses.

E. David's rise to power; end of Saul's reign (1 Sam 16:1–2 Sam 1:27)

David, the eighth of Jesse's sons, is anointed at Bethlehem. Being quite charismatic and successful, he becomes a member of Saul's court and moves into a position to threaten his power.

In chapter 17 David fights with a Philistine champion named Goliath. With the skill of a shepherd boy who becomes a warrior, he kills the Philistine with a stone slung from his slingshot. Seeing that their champion is dead, the Philistines flee, with the Israelites in hot pursuit and shouting after them.

David's rise to power continues (ch. 18). The anger of Saul is soon aroused when the militia return with David from fighting the Philistines and the women from the towns of Israel go out to meet Saul singing "Saul has killed his thousands, and David his ten thousands" (v. 7). From that day on, Saul "eyes" David with suspicion and jealousy.

In the large body of material in 1 Samuel 18:6–31:13 there are at least five factors and developments that contribute to David's rise to power while Saul's power degenerates.

- the work of an "evil spirit" in Saul (16:14), including his massacre of the priests at Nob (ch. 22)
- the friendship and support of Jonathan (18:1-4; 20:8, 16; 23:18)
- David's marriages: to Saul's daughter Michal (18:20-30); to Abigail (ch. 25); to Ahinoam (25:43), possibly a wife of Saul
- the successful establishment of a power base in the south (22:1-4), including becoming a Philistine vassal chieftain assigned to the town of Ziklag (27:1-7)
- help from Samuel at critical points (19:18-24); includes the post-mortem appearance of Samuel to Saul with the female medium at Endor (ch. 28)

Most of 2 Samuel 1 is composed of David's elegy of lament and praise for Saul and Jonathan after their death on Mt. Bilboa (ch. 31). There seems to be no good reason to doubt that David feels real grief regarding Saul and Jonathan; it is quite plausible to think that he personally never intended to supplant either Saul or Jonathan in the kingship.

II. David's reign (1000-950 BCE) (2 Sam 2:1–24:25)

A. King of Judah (2:1–4:12)

David goes to Hebron under a divine commission, taking with him his wives, his men, and their families. He is anointed king of Judah by the people. He reaches across the Jordan River with a message of blessing and promise of reward for the people of Jabesh-Gilead, because of their burial of Saul. The Philistines do not interfere.

Ishbaal, a son of Saul, is established as king at Mahanaim, over an assortment of northern and east Jordan tribes, and supported by Abner, commander of Saul's army. Hostilities between the house of Saul and the house of David continue for a long time, with David growing stronger and the Saulides growing weaker.

B. King of all Israel (5:1–12:31)

David consolidates his reign with the capture of Jerusalem and the centralization of Yahweh worship. At Hebron, the elders of the tribes anoint him as king over all Israel.

1. (5:17-25) The Philistines are defeated after they move to attack David.
2. (6:1-23) David moves the ark of God from Abinadab's house on the hill to Jerusalem. Uzzah, one of the men driving the cart, is struck dead when he reaches out and takes hold of the ark when the oxen pulling the cart on which it is being carried stumble, apparently a ritual mishap (cf. 1 Chron 15:1-15).
3. (7:1-29) David's "house" is legitimated, but he is not allowed to build a temple for the ark of God. This chapter serves as a kind of theological charter for the Davidic

monarchy. David's proposal to build a temple for Yahweh, made at his own initiative and without divine
commission, is rejected. However, Yahweh promises to
build a "house" for David, primarily a dynasty that will
have perpetuity: "Your house and your throne shall be
made sure forever before me" (v. 16a). The Davidic king
is given the status of divine sonship: "I will be a father to
him, and he shall be a son to me" (v. 14).

4. (8:1–9:13) David's armies defeat the Philistines, Moabites, Arameans, Edomites, and other groups. He sets up
   an extensive administrative structure over his kingdom.
5. (10:1-19; 11:1; 12:26-31) David's armies defeat the
   Arameans and Ammonites. David is at the apex of his
   power, with a huge crown of milcom on his head.
6. (11:1–12:25) David commits adultery with Bathsheba,
   plots the death of Uriah, and is judged by the prophet
   Nathan. The first child born to Bathsheba and David
   dies. Later their second child, Solomon, is born.

C. Domestic and political troubles (13:1–20:26)

Chapters 15–18 focus on the revolt of Absalom and David's
flight from Jerusalem. The core passages are framed by
chapters 13-14, which tells the story of discord in Absalom's family and his rise to prominence, and by chapters
19–20, which contain accounts of David's return to
Jerusalem and the revolt of Sheba.

1. (13:1-39) Ammon rapes Tamar, Absalom's sister;
   Absalom retaliates.
2. (14:1-24) Joab provokes Absalom's return to Jerusalem
   by enlisting the help of a wise woman from Tekoa.
3. (14:25-33–19:8a) Absalom steals the hearts of the people
   (15:6) and revolts against David in an attempt to take
   the throne. Absalom is killed by Joab and his men.
4. (19:8b–20:3) David returns to Jerusalem.
5. (20:4-22) Sheba's revolt is squelched. Joab murders
   Amasa.
6. (20:23-26) Listed among David's high officials are Joab,
   commander of the army; Jehoshaphat, recorder; and
   Zadok and Abiathar, priests.

D. A Davidic collection of varied accounts (21–24)

III. David's final days; succession of Solomon (1 Kgs 1:1–2:12)

A. Abishag, the Shunammite, cares for David, who is losing his physical power (1:1-4).
B. Adonijah, a son of David, tries to take the throne (1:5-10).
C. Nathan and Bathsheba plot and successfully persuade David to decide for Solomon as his successor (1:11-31).
D. Solomon ascends to the throne (1:32-53).
E. Before dying, David gives a final charge to Solomon, which reflects the best and the worst of David (2:1-12).

IV. Solomon's reign (950–930 BCE) (1 Kgs 2:13–11:43)

This long narrative has sections, but it is clearly centered around the building of the temple (chs. 5–8). It is placed between a complex account of Solomon's reign in chapters 3–4 and 9–11. Sections on the adversaries, or potential adversaries, of Solomon frame the entire account in 2:13-46 and 11:14-43. Within the larger narrative, the marriages of Solomon to foreign women frame 3:1-3 and 11:1-13.

A. Prologue (2:13–3:3)

Under the direction of Bathsheba, Nathan, Benaiah, and Zadok: Adonijah is executed; the priest Abiathar is banished to Anathoth; Joab and Shimei are executed; the kingdom is established in the hand of Solomon (2:46b).

B. Gift of Wisdom (3:4–4:34)

Accounts of Solomon's wisdom are given in 3:4-15 and 4:29-34. This section displays the two-sidedness of Solomon, who loves Yahweh and conforms to the precepts of his father David. But he allows the people to worship and participates with them at the "high places," where idolatry grows rampantly under the influence of Solomon's foreign wives. Still, Solomon's great wisdom, a gift from God is displayed and becomes renowned.

C. Building the temple (5:1–9:9)

1. (5:1-18) Solomon receives massive assistance for building the temple from Hiram, king of Tyre, a former ally of David (see 2 Sam 5:11-12; 5:1-18).

2. (6:1–7:51) Actual building of the temple is described. The project is said to have begun in the fourth year of Solomon's reign, designated as 480 years after the exodus of the Israelites from Egypt. Numbers are not exact, and many conclude that the numbers here and elsewhere are round-figure estimates denoting a certain number of generations rather than a specific number of 365-day-long years, but the date is about 966–960 BCE.

3. (8:1-66) This narrative begins with an account of the movement of the ark into the temple, including a description of the cloud of the glory of Yahweh filling the temple ("house"), so that the priests have to stop their ministering. The ark, the tent of meeting, and the holy vessels in the tent are all brought up to the temple. The text is not explicit, but it is quite possible that the tent shrine, with the ark and holy vessels in it, was installed in the temple. Indeed, this may be the tabernacle (see Commentary and Reflection). The ark is placed in the inner sanctuary, the holy of holies, under the wings of the cherubim. Possibly all of this is in the tent-tabernacle inside the temple. An oracle attributed to Solomon, in verses 12-13, affirms that he has built an "exalted house" for Yahweh "to dwell in forever." The prayer in verses 22-53 is the centerpiece of the narrative. The great festival described in verses 65-66 was the fall festival of Tabernacles.

4. (9:1-9) Yahweh appears to Solomon a second time, with explicit reference to the appearance at Gibeon in chapter 3. The message is a two-sided response to Solomon's prayer in chapter 8, and in a sense to all he has done in chapters 3–8. On the positive side, Yahweh declares that his prayer has been heard, and that the temple has been consecrated, made holy and set apart for God, and that the divine Name has been put there permanently—"My eyes and my heart will be there for all time" (9:3; better,

"continually"). On the negative side, the message warns
that if there is failure in the strict faithfulness demanded
of Solomon and his successors, the temple will be
destroyed, regardless of the fact that it is "the house that
I have consecrated for my name" (v. 7), and Israel will
be "cut off from the land."

D. Wise rule (9:10–10:29)

1. (9:10-28) Solomon institutes an extensive building
   program.
2. (9:15-22) Solomon uses forced labor.
3. (9:23-28) Some of Solomon's domestic and commercial
   activities are summarized.
4. (10:1-29) The queen of Sheba visits, bearing great riches
   and inquiring of Solomon's wisdom and prosperity.
   They exchange much wealth. Solomon is at the apex of
   his wealth and "wisdom." His extravagance is un-
   bounded, with a great throne of ivory overlaid with gold.

E. End of reign (11:1-43)

1. (11:1-13) These verses form a framing narrative with
   3:1-3, both focused on Solomon's wives and his building
   projects, with reference to the high places of worship.
   The Deuteronomistic review of Solomon's reign in
   verses 9-13 yields a negative verdict: he has not kept the
   covenant and its stipulations, thus "I will surely tear the
   kingdom from you and give it to your servant" (v. 13).
   The blame for Solomon's failure is placed on his foreign
   wives, an Egyptian princess being the first mentioned
   (3:1; 7:8).
2. (11:14-25) External adversaries suddenly enter the
   depiction of Solomon's reign. The term "satan" for
   "adversary" or "opponent" comes into play. Two satans
   are mentioned: Hadad, an Edomite leader, who appears
   as a Joseph-like figure who prospers for a time in Egypt,
   and Rezon, a David-like marauder who becomes the
   king of Damascus.
3. (11:26-40) Internal opposition to Solomon arises in the
   person of Jeroboam, son of Nebat.

4. (11:41-43) Solomon dies and is succeeded by his son Rehoboam.

V.   Revolt by the northern tribes against Rehoboam; division of the kingdom (1 Kgs 12:1-19)

VI. Kings of the divided kingdoms (1 Kgs 12:20–2 Kgs 17:41)

This large section of Samuel-Kings is composed of numerous subsections of material, but the framework is provided by the stereotyped summaries of the reigns of individual kings. In most cases there is an introductory résumé, or summary, of the reign. At the end there is a concluding regal résumé. The stylized summaries of each reign serve as literary vehicles for the treatment of the reigns of the kings without becoming overloaded with details.

The chronology of the kings is a complex subject that is plagued by problems of matching events with dates from external sources and by gaps and mismatching of chronology in the biblical accounts. Modern scholars have given the matter much attention, but without sure results. The dates used in the material that follows are largely those associated with the work of Edwin R. Thiele (*The Mysterious Numbers of the Hebrews Kings*). They are close to correct.

A. Jeroboam (930–909 BCE) (1 Kgs 12:20–14:20)

1. (12:20) Jeroboam is made king by the assembly at Shechem, with no support from those committed to the Davidic dynasty.
2. (12:21-24) Rehoboam mobilizes Judah for war against Israel in order to restore his rule of the lost territory. The effort is aborted by a prophet named Shemaiah.
3. (12:25-32) Jeroboam rebuilds Shechem and Penuel and establishes Bethel and Dan as worship centers for the northern kingdom.
4. (12:33–13:34) Jeroboam goes to the altar he had made at Bethel during festival time. Then a strange story is told about a prophet from Judah and a prophet from Bethel.
5. (14:1-20) Ahijah prophesies at Shiloh against Jeroboam. Jeroboam's reign is summarized.

B. Rehoboam in Judah (930–913 BCE) (1 Kgs 14:21-31)

Rehoboam's reign is summarized; Judah is said to have done evil in the sight of Yahweh during his reign. A historical account of the invasion of King Shishak of Egypt is inserted in verses 25-28.

C. Abijam (913–910 BCE) and Asa in Judah (910-869 BCE) (1 Kgs 15:1-24)

Abijam is judged negatively, as not being "true to the Lord his God, like the heart of his father David" (v. 3). He is granted the favor of a successor for David's sake. Asa reigns for 41 years and appears as a reformer of worship in Jerusalem. He removes male prostitutes and idols from the temple and removes the Queen Mother, Maacah, because she made an image for Asherah. The reform seems to be incomplete, however, and restricted to interests in Jerusalem.

D. Nadad (909–908 BCE), Baasha (908–886 BCE), and Elah in Israel (1 Kgs 15:25–16:8)

Nadad rules for two years until Baasha assassinates him.

E. Omri (885–874 BCE) and Ahab in Israel (874–853 BCE) (1 Kgs 16:8–22:40)

1. (16:8-29) The reign of Omri begins with Elah's assassination by Zimri, who reigns only seven days, but during that time he fulfills prophecy by destroying the house of Baasha. He is killed in a coup led by Omri, commander of the army. Omri is made king by all Israel when the news spreads. Omri reigns at Tirzah for six years and at Samaria for six years.

2. (16:29-34) Ahab's reign begins. He marries Jezebel, a daughter of Ethbaal, king of Sidon, and erects an altar for Baal in "in the house of Baal, which he built in Samaria" (v. 32). He makes an Asherah, a "sacred pole" representing the goddess Asherah, a consort of Baal.

3. (17:1-7) Elijah, a Tishbite from Gilead, appears suddenly with a message for Ahab.

4. (17:8-16) Elijah journeys to Zarephath on the Phoenician coast out of the territory of Ahab. Two incidents relating to a widow there are told.
5. (18:1-46) Elijah triumphs over the prophets of Baal on Mount Carmel.
6. (19:1-18) Elijah flees to Mount Horeb and experiences the presence of Yahweh in a cave and learns that his mission is not finished.
7. (20:1-43) Accounts are given of the words and actions of unnamed prophets in war between King Benhadad of Aram and King Ahab of Israel.
8. (21:1-29) The story is told of Naboth and his vineyard at Jezreel beside the palace of King Ahab.
9. (22:1-38) Israel is at war with Aram (Syria). Three years of peace between the two are broken by a joint venture between King Jehoshaphat of Judah and Ahab to retake Ramoth-Gilead, controlled by the Arameans. Ahab dies in the battle.
10. (22:39-40) Ahab builds an "ivory house" for himself.

F. Reign of the Omride dynasty (1 Kgs 22:41–2 Kgs 11:21): Jehoshaphat of Judah (872–848 BCE); Ahaziah (853–852 BCE), Jehoram (852–841 BCE), and Jehu (841–814 BCE) of Israel; Athaliah of Judah (841–835 BCE)

1. (1 Kgs 22:41-50) The account of the reign of Jehoshaphat of Judah is accompanied with brief historical notes.
2. (1 Kgs 22:51–2 Kgs 1:18) The reign of Ahaziah of Israel, son of Ahab, is marked by a narrative regarding Elijah's intervention in the king's attempt to recover from a fall at the palace in Samaria. Ahaziah's reign is judged to be "evil": he serves Baal and provokes Yahweh to anger.
3. (2 Kgs 2:1–8:29) The work of Elisha and the reign of Jehoram of Israel are described. The pattern of fitting the activities of prophets into the reigns of kings subordinates the activities of the kings to those of the prophets, with the summaries of the kings providing a framework for the accounts of the prophets.
   a) (2:1-26) The transfer of leadership from Elijah to Elisha is an explanation of the departure of Elijah, but celebrates his legacy left behind with Elisha.

b) (3:1-8:15) Two thematic concepts in the prologue formed by chapter 2 are woven into the passages that follow: (1) prophets as agents of healing and (2) prophets as agents of prophecy and military power.

(1) prophets as agents of healing

> (*a*) (2:19-22) Elisha asks for a new bowl, uncontaminated and suitable for ritual, and for salt to symbolize the removal of a curse from a spring. The bad spring impacts the whole region with death and miscarriage. The "healing" of the water is the means of healing the people.

> (*b*) (4:1-7) Elisha does a wonder act parallel to that of Elijah in 1 Kings 17:14-16. This is the first of a series of stories setting forth the power of a prophet to perform wondrous deeds. Healing has broad dimensions, especially in connection with food supplies, famine, and social distress. Sickness is not confined to the physical condition of an individual's unwellness.

> (*c*) (4:8-37) The Shunamite woman's son is healed.

> (*d*) (4:38-41) The prophetic community at Gilgal is involved in this account of the contamination of a pot of stew by the mistake of gathering and cooking a poisonous plant. Elisha has meal (flour) thrown into the pot, which neutralizes the "death of the pot" so they can eat the stew.

> (*e*) (4:42-44) Food comes to Elisha by a man from a place called Baal-shalishah, probably 10-15 miles west-southwest of Shechem, whose servant is ordered by Elisha to give food to the people and let them eat.

> (*f*) (5:1-27) Naaman, the Aramean army commander, is healed. Elisha's servant, Gehazi, is afflicted with leprosy.

> (*g*) (6:1-7) The prophetic community is in need of more building space. Going to the Jordan Valley to cut logs for a new building, a borrowed ax head falls into the water, much to the distress of the prophet who lost it. Elisha cuts a stick, throws it into the water where the ax head fell,

and brings it to the surface. A crisis is solved. This is hardly healing in the normal sense, but there is a cry of distress; the community has a problem and healing of a sort is needed.

(*h*) (8:1-6) Warned by Elisha of an approaching seven-year famine, the Shunammite woman goes to Philistine territory for the duration of the famine, and her property is given back to her after she returns.

(2) prophets as agents of prophecy and military power

(*a*) (3:4-27) Jehoram of Israel stages a campaign against King Mesha of Moab. Elisha's wonder-working makes the campaign a success.

(*b*) (6:8-23) Elisha's military prowess as an agent of Yahweh is demonstrated against an invasion from Aram.

(*c*) (6:24–7:20) The famine at Samaria, caused by a siege of the city by King Ben-hadad of Aram, ends when Yahweh causes the Aramean army to retreat.

(*d*) (8:7-15) Elisha is powerful in Damascus. He becomes involved with ailing King Ben-hadad of Aram. Hazael, a general or court official, is sent to Elisha with a gift of all kinds of goods (40 camel loads!) to ask almost the exact question that Ahaziah of Israel had sent to ask of Baal-zebub, the god of Ekron, in 2 Kings 1: "Will I recover from this illness?" However, Elisha's answer lacks the clarity of Elijah's definite "You shall surely die." Elisha says, "Go, say to him, 'You shall certainly recover'; but the Lord has shown me that he shall certainly die" (8:10). We may understand his statement as meaning that the king will recover from his illness but die soon. When Hazael returns to the king, he gives only part of the message from Elisha: "He told me that you would certainly recover" (8:14).

4. (8:16-29) The summaries of the reigns of Jehoram in
   Israel and Ahaziah in Judah contain brief historical
   notes regarding a revolt by Edom and the wounding of
   Jehoram in battle with the Arameans at Ramoth-gilead.
5. (9:1–11:21) Jehu stages a coup. Athaliah, a daughter of
   Ahab and the mother of Ahaziah of Judah, takes power
   in Jerusalem. The priest, Jehoida, leads a revolt again
   Athaliah, bringing an end to the Omride dynasty.

   a) (9:1-37) The prophet Elisha commissions Jehu to be
      king. Jehu bursts onto the scene as a divinely commis-
      sioned agent of judgment upon the northern kings.
      Note: the young prophet's message in 9:8-9 includes
      the whole house of Ahab, which is to be like the
      condemned houses of Jeroboam and Baasha.

   b) (10:1-27) Jehu continues his purge in Samaria and
      Jezreel. He arranges for the execution of the royal
      families of Jehoram and Ahaziah of Judah, receiving
      their heads in baskets and displaying them at the
      entrance of the gate of Jezreel. On his way to Samaria,
      Jehu has slaughtered 41 members of the household of
      Ahaziah on their way to visit their kin in Samaria.
      Joined by Johonadab son of Rechab (vv. 15-17), Jehu
      carries out a terrible purge of the worshipers of Baal,
      collecting a large assembly at the temple of Baal in
      Samaria, seemingly for a celebration of a great sac-
      rifice that he purports to be ready to offer to Baal.
      When the sacrifice is completed, Jehu's troops
      slaughter all the Baal worshipers and destroy the Baal
      temple built by Ahab (see 1 Kgs 16:32), making it "a
      latrine to this day." Thus Jehu has come to power over
      the corpses of his adversaries, finally purging the hill
      of Samaria of its Baalist worship, but at a high price.

   c) (10:28-36) Because Jehu wiped out Baal worship from
      Israel, he is promised a four-generation dynasty. But
      because he did not follow the law of God, he is given a
      negative judgment.His ruthless zeal against the Baal-
      ites does not save him from the sins of Jeroboam in
      maintaining a divided worship and country. During
      Jehu's reign, Yahweh begins to trim off parts of Israel,
      using Hazael and the Arameans as His agents.

d) (11:1-21) Athaliah is removed from power in Jerusalem by a coup d'etat arranged by the priest Jehoiada.

G. The reigns of Jehoash (Joash) (835–796 BCE), Jehoahaz (814–798 BCE), Jehoash (798–782 BCE), Jeroboam II (793–753 BCE), Amaziah (796–767 BCE), Azariah-Uzziah (792–740 BCE), Jotham (750–732 BCE) Ahaz (735–732 BCE), Hoshea (732–723/22 BCE); fall of the northern kingdom (2 Kgs 12:1–17:41)

1. (12:1-21) Jehoash of Judah does what is right in the sight of God, but is assassinated by his servants, likely at the urging of the temple priests. In general, the reign of Jehoash is presented as positive, despite his failures, but there is always in Kings "an eye to the ultimate insufficiency" of the kings to spare Israel from judgment.

2. (13:1–14:29) This canonical unit is framed by the summary of the reign of Joash (Jehoash) of Judah and the initial résumé of Azariah, son of Amaziah of Judah. The larger narrative covers the reigns of four kings: two in Israel and two in Judah. Jeroboam's restoration of the borders of Israel is said to be in accord with the word of Yahweh spoken by the prophet Jonah son of Amittai from Gath-hepher. This is the same name of the man associated with the book of Jonah, although that book has no indication of Jonah's role in 2 Kings 14:25. (Jonah is never specifically called a prophet in the book known by his name.) Amos, who belongs to the time of Jeroboam II, is not mentioned in Kings, possibly because he condemned the confidence of Jeroboam in his conquest of the Transjordan. There are two brief stories about the prophet Elisha in 13:14-19 and 13:20-21, the latter about the power of Elisha's bones after his death.

3. (15:1-38) The summary of Azariah's reign brings the differently organized material in chapters 13-14 into line with the synchronization of the reigns of the kings. The stable reigns of Azariah (also called Uzziah) and Jotham in Judah form a frame around the end of the Jehu dynasty and the disturbed period that follows in the northern kingdom. Assyria (in areas of modern Iran,

Iraq, Russia, and Turkey) becomes a major threat. A line of kings, beginning with Tiglath-pileser III (744–727 BCE), carry out a program of political and economic expansion and control of countries outside their traditional territory, including an empire that covers most of the Eastern Mediterranean seaboard. The Assyrians seek to develop policies for the relocation of population groups and the establishment of conquered territories in their system of provinces, with the payment of tribute. They expand into Syria-Palestine to control trade routes and commerce in order to gain a flow of goods and wealth into Assyria proper, and to control a threat to Assyria and Assyrian interests from a kingdom north of Assyria known as Urartu. The political and military dominance of the Assyrians is a major factor in Israelite history from 744 BCE until the collapse of Assyrian power in 612–609 BCE. The expansion of Assyrian power into Palestine energizes the Egyptians to resist and seek to dominate the same territory, so that there are continual back-and-forth movements during the Assyrian period between Assyrian and Egyptian efforts to dominate in Syria-Palestine.

4. (2 Kgs 16:1-20) The reign of Ahaz receives a strongly negative evaluation in 2 Kings, 2 Chronicles, and Isaiah. Isaiah presents him as the king of contrast to Hezekiah. Unlike Ahaz, Hezekiah is faithful and obedient.

5. (2 Kgs 17:1-41) The northern kingdom falls.

   a) (17:1-6) The reign of Hoshea and the fall of Samaria to the Assyrians are recounted.

   b) (17:7-23) The theological analysis of the fall and exile of the northern kingdom in these verses is one of the most significant sections in the book of Kings. Ten of the twelve tribes that entered the promised land of Promise go into permanent exile. The disaster in the north is attributed to the sin of the people and their worship of other gods, along with their walking "in the customs of the nations whom the Lord drove out" before them and by "customs that the kings of Israel had introduced" (v. 8). Verses 13-14 recall that Yahweh warned Israel and Judah by "every prophet and seer" who sought to turn them away from their destructive ways and toward obedience to the commandments of Yahweh's *torah* ("instruction") given to their ancestors and delivered by the prophets. However, the Israelites would not listen and continued in the stubborn ways of their ancestors. Thus they have rejected the commandments and the covenant made with their ancestors, along with the warnings Yahweh gave them.

(1) The kings play a major role, but the Israelites cannot blame the real failure of the nation on the monarchy; the people are responsible, too.

(2) The fall of Israel and the exile of the Israelites are the work of Yahweh; they are not due to the superior strength of foreign powers and their gods. Israel must deal with Yahweh regarding the exile. The gods of the foreign states are worthless.

c) (17:24-41) The historical narrative returns, with attention given to the deportation of Israelites by the Assyrians and the settlement of foreigners in the towns of Samaria (now an Assyrian province) where the Israelites had lived. A strange story follows. Yahweh sends lions among the newly settled people, and some of them are killed. The king of Assyria decides that the problem stems from the people's failure to "know the law of the god of the land" (v. 26). One of the exiled Israelite priests is sent to live among the newly settled people and teach them this law.

VII. Judah from the fall of the Northern Kingdom to the Babylonian exile (2 Kgs 18–25)

A. Hezekiah (726–697 BCE) (2 Kgs 18:1–20:21)

The book of Kings judges the reign of Hezekiah favorably. The contrast between the negative evaluation of Ahaz and the positive judgment of Hezekiah is striking. Ahaz does not do what is right in the sight of Yahweh, but Hezekiah does and is described as "holding fast to Yahweh" and keeping the commandments given to Moses. Because Yahweh is with him, he prospers wherever he goes.

1. (18:1-36) Hezekiah reforms worship. (see 2 Chron 29:3–31:21 for a detailed description).

2. (19:1–20:21) Beyond his direct actions to reorganize and purify worship, Hezekiah sets an example by his behavior, faith, and theology. He does not break under the taunts and threats of the Assyrians and sends to the prophet Isaiah for help. Throughout the crisis he is responsive to the messages of the prophet. In a striking incident (19:14-19), he takes a letter from Assyrian messengers to the temple and spreads it out before Yahweh, with a superb prayer of lament. The Assyrian envoys challenge Hezekiah and his people at crucial points of faith: his "trust/faith" in Yahweh; "your god" vs. "the gods of the nations"; "Shall you be delivered?" Hezekiah does not waver on any point; he exemplifies the way Israelites should respond to any crisis brought about by confrontation with world powers. The Assyrian king, Sennacherib, thinks he has written for the eyes of Hezekiah, but Hezekiah insists he has written for the eyes of Yahweh (19:16). True, the Assyrians have destroyed nations and their gods, but their gods are "no gods but the work of human hands—wood and stone" (v. 18). Yahweh is the "living God" and the only God worth having, the only God who can save.

B. Manasseh (697–642 BCE) and Amon (642–640 BCE) (2 Kgs 21:1-26)

1. (21:1-18) The initial summary of Manasseh's reign contains "an avalanche of negative comments" (House, 377) about his kingship. The opening evaluation, "He did what was evil in the sight of the Lord" (v. 2), is a positive form of the negative evaluation of Ahaz in 16:2: "He did not do what was right in the sight of the Lord." Manasseh is convicted on two points: he carries out a program like that of King Ahab of Israel and causes the people to do more evil than the nations destroyed by Yahweh before the Israelites. Manasseh is described as the direct opposite of the ideal king in Deuteronomic theology, leading the people in illegitimate worship

practices in Jerusalem and at illegitimate places. Of all
the kings, Manasseh is deemed the worst. Despite the
story of his conversion in 2 Chronicles (33:11-20), he is
left unredeemed in the book of Kings, and remains as
the arch representative of the doomed monarchy.

2. (21:19-26) Amon's reign is presented as a continuation
of the policies of his father Manasseh. His servants conspire and assassinate him, but the "people of the land"
intervene and execute Amon's killers, installing his
young son, Josiah, as king.

C. Josiah (640–609 BCE) (2 Kgs 22:1–23:30)

The account of Josiah's reign begins with a positive assessment of the character of his rule: "He did what was right in
the sight of the Lord . . . he did not turn aside to the right
or to the left" (22:2). The concluding summary of his kingship declares praise like that given of Hezekiah in chapter
18: "Before him there was no king like him, who turned to
the Lord with all his heart, with all his soul, and with all
his might, according to all the law of Moses; nor did any
like him arise after him" (23:25). The tone shifts, however,
in the account of Josiah's death, due to Manasseh's reign:
"The Lord did not turn from the fierceness of his great
wrath . . . because of all the provocations with which
Manasseh had provoked him. . . . I will remove Judah also
out of my sight, as I have removed Israel," including the
rejection of Jerusalem and the temple (23:26-29).

Josiah's reign ends when he is killed at Megiddo by the
Egyptian king Neco (609 BCE). He is then brought in a
chariot to Jerusalem for burial. The death of Josiah is an
unexpected one for a king praised so highly, and a theological shock. According to the theology of the book of
Deuteronomy, such a king should have been blessed with a
long reign and a peaceful death in his old age.

D. The last Davidic kings: Jehoahaz (609 BCE), Jehoiakim (609–598 BCE), Jehoiachin (598–597 BCE), Zedekiah (597–586 BCE); exile of Judah (2 Kgs 23:31–25:30)

The reigns of the four final Davidic kings of Judah are each marked by initial summaries, but only Jehoiakim is provided with the usual closing summary. This literary feature marks the troubled conditions of the last 22 years of Judah's life before exile. An epilogue deals with the governorship of Gedaliah and the treatment of Jehoichin in Babylon.

1. (23:31-35) The "people of the land" make the young Jehoahaz, a son of Josiah, king in Jerusalem after the death of his father. However, the Egyptians, led by Pharaoh Neco, are in control and take Jehoahaz from the throne after three months, confine him as a prisoner at Riblah, and impose heavy tribute on the land.

2. (23:36–24:7) Neco makes Eliakim, another son of Josiah, his puppet king in Jerusalem and gives him the throne name of Jehoiakim. Jehoiakim's reign in Jerusalem is characterized as "evil in the sight of Yahweh" and no better than his ancestors. Assyrian control in Palestine has lessened, and Egyptian control is established. However, the Egyptians are not able to prevail against the rising power of the Babylonians and are defeated in battles near and around Carchemish in 606–605, and subsequently are forced out of Syria and Palestine back to their homeland. Somehow Jehoiakim survives this debacle and is left in power by the Babylonians after they take control. He probably never gives up his confidence in Egypt, and after three years or so he rebels against the Babylonians, probably in the form of withholding tribute. The Babylonians do not take immediate action against Jehoiachim, but promote raids into Judah by various groups. Apparently, Jehoiakim dies during this period. (For more information on Jehoiakim, see Jer 22:1-30; 36:1-32).

3. (24:8-17) Jehoiachin, son of Jehoiakim, is almost immediately hit by a full-fledged siege in 597 BCE of Jerusalem by the Babylonians, led by Nebuchadnezzar. Jehoiachin surrenders, and he and his mother and his court are taken as prisoners to Babylon. The temple and palace are looted, and varied groups of people are gradually

deported to Babylonia. The Babylonians take away military people, skilled workers, and leaders, leaving the poorest people of the land behind.

4. (24:18–25:21) The Babylonians install Mattaniah, Jehoiakim's uncle and another son of Josiah, as king in place of Jehoaichin, changing his name to Zedekiah. His mother, Hamutal, is also the mother of Jehoahaz. He receives the same negative evaluation as Manasseh, Amon, Jehoaikim, and Jehoiachin. He rebels against the king of Babylon in the ninth year of his reign, leading to a Babylonian attack against Jerusalem and its subsequent destruction. The temple and "all the houses" (important buildings?) of Jerusalem are burned, and the walls are broken down. Special attention is given to the looting of the gold and bronze vessels and the furnishings of the temple, along with the two pillars, the sea (see 1 Kgs 7:22-26), and the stands and decorative work. Zedekiah attempts to escape from the doomed city, but the Babylonians apprehend him swiftly, and he is arrested and taken to Nebuchadnezzar at Riblah. There he is tried and sentenced to a cruel punishment: his sons are slaughtered before him, his eyes are put out, then he is bound in fetters and taken to Babylon. Seventy-one religious and civil leaders are taken by Nebuzaradan, captain of the Babylonian guard, to Nebuchadnezzar's headquarters at Riblah where they are executed. These leaders include the chief priest Seraiah and the second priest Zephaniah. The narrative ends on a note of finality: "So Judah went into exile out of its land" (25:21).

5. (25:22-30) Gedaliah is appointed governor of the people who remain in the land, stationed at Mizpah, about five miles north of Jerusalem. He is from a family of leadership, a son of Ahikam (2 Kgs 22:12; 40:5-10), and receives support from Jeremiah and other leaders and groups, but soon is assassinated by a man named Ishmael and his men. After Gedaliah's death, a contingent of people trek to Egypt, taking Jeremiah (25:26; Jer 41–43) with them against his will. The book of Kings closes with a note about the release from prison of King Jehoiachin of Judah. A curtain of divine judgment has

fallen across the history of Israel, but there is at least a small door open to the future. The release of the Davidic king in Babylon, partial as it is, is a clue that Yahweh has not forgotten His people or deserted His loyalty to them. Jehoiachin is permitted to have only limited freedom in Babylon, but he puts off his prison clothes and eats his bread before the king. He lives, and so does Israel, even in exile.

Commentary and Reflection

The personalities of Saul and David dominate the text of the books of Samuel. Their lives and careers are so intertwined that "in life and in death they were not divided" (2 Sam 1:23). The intertwining of their lives also involves Samuel, who binds the two together in life and in death.

I. Saul

The Saul who appears in the narratives of the book of Samuel has provoked divergent judgments regarding his character and the nature of his career. Frequently he has been evaluated in terms of tragic failure, inspiring in those who read about him a mix of "pity and terror." If he is evaluated from the perspective of the tragic, the emphasis will be upon his strength and the paradox of the weakness of strength. The weak who perish in frustration and confusion are not tragic; they are simply weak and ineffective.

In recent literature, J. P. Fokkelman has argued for a tragic interpretation of Saul, calling him "a tragic hero." According to Fokkelmann, Saul suffers from the "crossed fates" of Samuel, David, and himself. He is the victim of the careers of Samuel and David and of "a God whose rationality is beyond our ken." Fokkelmann recognizes the weaknesses in Saul but argues that, despite his terrible record, it is possible for the reader to feel sympathy for him. Saul has the misfortune of not being prepared for the monarchy, and he breaks under heavy theocratic demands that can hardly be satisfied. In addition, Samuel's manipulation of prophecy may add to our sympathy for Saul, who is used, undermined, and discarded for another.

Along these lines, the argument that Saul is a sacrifice may have merit. In this interpretation he becomes a surrogate for the people, deflecting divine wrath from the nation and making possible the transition to kingship in the Davidic monarchy. According to Daniel Hawk ("Saul as Sacrifice," *Bible Review*, 1996), Saul is the necessary sacrifice for bringing about the transformation of Israel. This approach is built on the thesis that one of the basic functions of sacrifice is to serve some communal need, especially a need for peace and stability in times of social dissolution and turmoil. Thus, Hawk argues that Saul's death resolves the tension between leaving a divinely endorsed structure of Israelite society—a tribal confederacy led by charismatic judge/champions—for another divinely blessed social structure —the monarchy of David.

The book of 1 Samuel can be read as an attempt to resolve this tension, focused on the major characters of Samuel, Saul, and David. Samuel is the last of the judges of the old order, and David establishes the new order of a dynastic monarchy. Saul is caught in the "crossed fates," trying to be both a champion and a king and serving as a sacrifice that holds the nation together and permits Yahweh to go on with the divine work through Israel. Perhaps we should remember that Yahweh's purpose for Saul in 1 Samuel 9:16 is that "he shall save my people from the land of the Philistines; for I have seen the suffering of my people, because their outcry has come to me." As the high priest Caiphas is reported to have said, ironically, about Jesus: "It is better for you to have one man die for the people than to have the whole nation destroyed" (John 11:50). Does Saul die for his people?

The tragic aspect of Saul is strengthened by a purely historical analysis of his career, looking past the spiritual judgments in 1 Samuel. Saul appears as a brave and competent commander of relatively well-conducted military campaigns. He appears to have driven back an Ammonite threat east of the Jordan River and established Israelite control of the hill country west of the Jordan against the threat of Philistine occupation and power, saving the Israelites from Philistine conquest. His pursuit of David through Judah and the Negev may seem to be foolish and irrational, but in doing so he extends his dominance over the south and gains some support. His forcing of David into

Philistine territory tends to neutralize Philistine pressure in the south, whether the result is intended by Saul or not. The battle at Mount Gilboa produces a defeat for the Israelites and the death of Saul, but the Philistines do not seem to capitalize on the victory, whatever their exact intentions may be. Saul's reign also allows David to prepare himself for kingship in the south before extending his reign into the north. These are all positive aspects of Saul's reign.

On the other hand, it is not difficult to understand Saul as a failure, who incurrs the wrath of God. He is pictured as suffering from gross miscalculations, especially in his turning back from carrying out the terrible mission assigned to him by Yahweh in the matter of the Amalekites (see 1 Sam 15; 28; 31:18-19) and in the case of the massacre of the priests at Nob (1 Sam 22). He took his guidance from the people with disastrous results. Other biblical traditions share the view of the present text in 1 Samuel regarding Saul.

According to 1 Chronicles 10:13-14, Saul dies for his faithlessness. He does not keep the command of Yahweh. He consults a medium rather than seeking guidance from Yahweh. But according to 1 Samuel 28:6, Saul inquires of the Lord, but the Lord does not answer him, so he seeks guidance from a medium. Saul is not mentioned in the list of the heroes of Israel in Ecclesiasticus 46–50, whereas Samuel is praised highly (46:13-20). However, Acts 13:21-22 is more neutral toward Saul. Kenneth I. Cohen ("King Saul: A Bungler from the Beginning," *Bible Review*, 1994) judges Saul as a "preposterous choice for king" and his reign as "a catastrophe in statecraft," which was inferior even to that of the judges. Saul was "flawed from the outset" and was "God's revenge" for the people's rejection of Yahweh as king. Cohen argues that the biblical narrator presents Saul as "a hapless fool thrust into the kingship" as God's punishment of the Israelites for demanding a monarchy. This critique is too severe; the truth almost certainly lies somewhere between a "tragic hero" and "hapless fool."

Perhaps 1 Samuel 15:17 is the key to the depths of Saul's character. Samuel rebukes Saul for his conduct of the campaign against the Amalekites by saying, "Though you are little in your own eyes, are you not the head of the tribes of Israel? Yahweh anointed you king over Israel." The difficult language of this verse can be read with reference to a timid Saul in 9:21, but it seems justifiable to think in terms of a double meaning: "Though you were small in your own eyes you became the head of the tribes of Israel, and Yahweh anointed you as king, and you are still too small in your own eyes to be king, despite the fact that you are." The NJV translates the verse as "You may look small to yourself, but you are the head of the tribes of Israel." The REB has "Once you thought little of yourself, but now you are the head of the tribes of Israel," which implies that Saul still thinks too little of himself in his role as king.

The littleness in which Saul holds himself prevents him from actualizing the tough commitments and resoluteness of purpose demanded of the kingly role. Conceivably this is the source of the instability that entangles him repeatedly in *ad hoc* and destructive behavior. The "littleness" of his soul leads him into the desperate attempt to get protection from a dead Samuel through the female sorcerer at Endor (1 Sam 28:3-25), whom he leaves to go out into the night of death. We may conceivably feel a certain terror when we contemplate Saul because we know that, due to our own "unfaith," we fail to match our high calling with sufficient self-esteem. Saul causes us to tremble because of our own unfaith in the power of God to do through us what He has called us to be and do.

The role of Samuel in relation to Saul is difficult to fathom. Samuel brings Saul to power, as he does David, but he subverts the reign of Saul and finally pronounces a death sentence on him. Samuel grieves over Saul, a grief broken only when Yahweh calls him out of it for another mission, ironically to anoint another king-to-be.

We can hope that his grief is not wholly directed toward Saul, because Samuel should be grieving, at least in part, for his own undermining of Saul's kingship. We miss any effort to intervene with Yahweh on the part of Samuel for Saul. Maybe there is some exception to the failure of Samuel to pray for Saul in 1 Samuel 15:11, where Samuel is angry and cries out to Yahweh all night. But we are not told the subject of the anger, although the context suggests it is Saul, or the nature of the "crying out" to Yahweh. Is he simply lamenting his miserable condition, or is he "crying out" for mercy for Saul? Is he angry with Saul alone, or is he angry with *both* Saul and Yahweh?

After all, the choice of Saul was not his—indeed, the whole matter of kingship was against his will. Yahweh overrode his reluctance for the sake of Israel. The matter is veiled in ambiguity, as are most of the actions of Samuel.

In the case of Saul, Samuel declares that Yahweh does not change His mind—or at least Samuel does not intend to try to get Yahweh to do so. The statement is patently incorrect, since Yahweh plainly says in 15:11 that He has done so. Samuel is unwilling to put his life at risk in order to seek a change in Yahweh's intention; or, perhaps like Jonah in the case of Nineveh, he does not want Yahweh to relent and change his mind about Saul. The idea of an unchangeable God often meets deep needs in those who feel their power is threatened and who cringe before the theology of a God who responds to situations according to God's free will. Samuel needs what he perceives to be a rigidity in God's purpose that seems to offer certainty.

Perchance Samuel does nothing more subversive of Saul's well-being than to allow, indeed to encourage, him to become involved with ecstatic prophecy. In this case, Samuel should have warned Saul to have nothing to do with such prophets and their frenzied behavior. In the Old Testament, prophets accompany the monarchy all the way through its history. But prophets are not to usurp the power of kings and vice versa. Polzin argues correctly that no king, except for Saul, is ever called a prophet; kingship and prophecy are not to be united in the same person. The frenzy of the prophets destabilize Saul and give Samuel powerful leverage to humiliate him. With a prophet like Samuel, Saul hardly has a chance. No thoughtful reader can leave the accounts of Saul, Samuel, and David with an easy sense of well-being. The "crossed fates" of divine will and providence are certainly evident. Only God knows how to untangle the threads.

II. David

The appendix in 2 Samuel 21–24 provides a collection of material that serves as a sort of mosaic of David's career. McCarter's arrangement of the disparate material suggests a deliberate design: narrative (21:1-14), list (21:15-22), poem(s) (22:1-51; 23:1-7), list (23:8-39). The collection has a kaleidoscopic nature as it moves from one vignette, list, or poem to another. In his book *Power, Providence, and Personality*, Walter Brueggemann proposes that chapters 21–24 dismantle or deconstruct the picture of an extravagantly royal David and form a counterpart to his aggrandizing ways. In what follows, I am deeply indebted to Brueggemann's analysis.

On the surface David appears in an innocent and favorable light. A careful reading of the context, however, reveals ambivalence and ambiguity in his character and career. He appears with superb quality of character and leadership in the vignette of the water from the well of Bethlehem (23:13-17). Here David is in the field with his soldiers, at risk with his troops in battle, not back in the royal palace with servants and messengers to do his bidding. His power is that of loyalty and respect for his leadership, and his regard for the lives of his warriors is in sharp contrast to his cynical message to Joab in 2 Samuel 11:25. David is thirsty, sharing the needs of his people. On the other hand, the name of Uriah the Hittite appears at the end of the list of David's mighty men in 23:18-39. Uriah stands as a sentinel to remind us of the arrogance of power on the part of David as king, and reminds us that royal ideology is finally subordinated to the governance of Yahweh. "Do not let this matter trouble you" is David's message to Joab, but "this matter" is evil in the eyes of Yahweh.

The poems in 22:1-51 and 23:1-7 yield a mixed picture. The song of deliverance in 22:1-20 is marvelously focused on God and on the divine response to a call for help—a psalm of thanksgiving praise. However, 22:29-51 is a victory song that praises the speaker—assumed to be David—with excessive extravagance. The speaker declares that Yahweh has blessed him according to his righteousness: "according to the cleanness of my hands he recompensed me" (v. 21). Thus the speaker declares himself blameless before God and free of guilt (v. 24). Verses 21-25 are framed by use of the words righteousness, recompense, and cleanness. When these words are read as David's words late in his career, they have a hollow sound, and the repeated statements of personal strength and achievements (vv. 29-46), although attributed to divine empowerment, seem to reflect a vaunting of personal prowess. As Brueggemann says, all this comes "after David's story has played itself out." Reports of the virtuous David are less than convincing. Despite the narrator's judgment in 2 Samuel 8:15 that David "administered justice and equity (righteousness) to all his people," we know now that his career was not full of righteousness and "blamelessness." We know too many sordid details.

The poem in 2 Samuel 23:1-7 expresses a strong royal ideology focused on David: exalted by God, anointed to be the singer of Israel's psalms ("the favorite of the Strong One of Israel"), and the one through whom the spirit of Yahweh speaks. The king is described as the giver of life; like the light, like the sun, like the rain: "Is not my house like this with God?" (vv. 4-5). This is high kingship ideology and theology. However, there is a conditional element at the end of verse 3: the statements that follow are true when one rules over people justly (righteously) and in the "fear of God." The conditionality could be dismissed as stylistic if the psalm were not in its present context. But in chapters 21-24, the high claims of royal power are bent to the provisions that apply to every Israelite.

Each of the framing narratives in 21:1-14 and 25:1-25 have a dual view of David. In each case, the initial view is negative. The oracle David receives in 21:1 is a private one and seems to justify his action in satisfying the vengeance of the Gibeonites as a response to the divine will and necessary to relieve the famine. However, the oracle only links the famine to the blood-guilt of Saul and his family. There is no divine command for David to act, and after the oracle he negotiates with the Gibeonites on his own.

We can understand the concern of a king for his family and people during a time of famine, but there are other ways to deal with bloodguilt and famine. The Gibeonites themselves mention silver and gold (21:4), ostensibly rejecting it; nevertheless, it suggests an opening. Also, the Gibeonites declare that it is not "for us to put anyone to death in Israel." Although the meaning of this statement is not clear, it seems to provide an opening for negotiation that David does not pursue. The deal for the execution of seven sons of Saul is worked out by David and the Gibeonites without any sign of divine guidance. David removes potential rivals for his throne by his action, and he does so by taking advantage of old customs of bloodguilt to accomplish his political objectives. This act is probably the basis of Shimei's curse against David in 16:8—to which David responds, "The Lord has bidden him" (16:11), justifying the behavior of Shimei.

David appears in a much better light in the second half of the account in 2 Samuel 21:1-14, when he responds to the grief and persistence of Rizpah and arranges for an honorable burial of the sons of Saul slain by the Gibeonites, along with the bones of Saul and Jonathan brought back from Jabesh-Gilead. This is a portrayal of the king as concerned for the suffering of Rizpah and respectful of her loyalty. His actions are appropriate, but, of course, it is easier to honor the dead than to defend the living when they are your rivals. Incidentally, the seven sons are put to death in the first days of the barley harvest (21:9), but the drought is broken only later in the context of Rizpah's grief and the public mass burial by David (vv. 12-14): "After that, God heeded supplications for the land." The hangings by the Gibeonites have accomplished nothing for the land, however much they may have helped David politically.

The same pattern seems evident in the narrative of 2 Samuel 24:1-25. Yahweh is angry with Israel and motivates David to "count" the people of Israel and Judah. (1 Chronicles 21:1 has an agent of God called "satan," "an adversary," to rise in judgment on Israel and move David to "count" Israel; assuming possibly that Yahweh would have motivated David by the use of some agent—"satan" is not here the devil). We are not told why Yahweh is angry with Israel. This narrative has its counterpart in 21:1-14, and the anger of Yahweh has its counterpart in the famine of 21:1, which is related to a violation of an oath made to the Gibeonites, although there is no similar rationale stated for the anger in 24:1. The account reads as if it were extracted from a longer narrative we no longer have, only part of it being selected for use in chapter 24. In a loose intertextual manner, 24:1-25 follows chapters 22 and 23, with David securely established in his reign in Jerusalem and looking for ways to extend and enhance his power.

The divine anger remains a mystery, but it provides the context for David's census. He does not hesitate to order Joab and the commanders of the army to go through the territory of his kingdom to take a census. The NRSV properly changes the verb in verse 2 from that in verse 1, from "count the people" in verse 1 to "take a census of the people" in verse 2. Yahweh's command to "go count the people of Israel and Judah" is a rather neutral and inclusive term, meaning to count all the people. However, David interprets this as a "census" in the form of a "visitation," a going through and searching out in all the tribes of Israel.

In the ancient world a census taken by a king had two purposes, military draft and taxation, and was usually a form of official terrorism. The nature of the "visiting" ordered by David becomes clear when Joab reports to the king in terms of the numbers of "soldiers able to draw the sword"—800,000 + 500,000. Joab knows the danger of this action and seeks to dissuade the king from doing so, but he is overruled. David presses on with his plan, falling into the trap Yahweh has set for him. The numbering of Israel for the glory of Yahweh, whose people they are, has become an exercise of royal power. The census implicitly mobilizes the kingdom of David against the kingship of Yahweh. The huge number of potential soldiers runs counter to the Deuteronomic theology of war (see Deut 20:1-9 and the account of Gideon in Judg 7:1–8:35).

David knows he is in trouble when the census is over: "I have sinned greatly" (v. 10). However, he does not appear to be very noble when he chooses the punishment for his offense: "let *us* fall into the hand of Yahweh . . . but let *me* not fall into human hands" (v. 14). In other words, let the nation suffer, but don't let me flee for three months while my foes pursue me! His reference to the great mercy of Yahweh may be legitimate, but the "let us" versus "let me not" makes the reader suspicious that David is primarily concerned for himself. However that may be, David's response to the plague itself is superlative.

After Yahweh has relented about the evil and the angel who destroys the people stretches a hand out toward Jerusalem, David confesses, "I alone have sinned," and exonerates the "sheep" (people) of his realm: "Let your hand, I pray, be against me and against my father's house" (v. 17). The good shepherd-king is willing to lay down his life for the sheep-people. He sounds almost like Moses interceding for the sinful Israelites. This could be David at his best. Now he proceeds to build an altar in Jerusalem for the worship of Yahweh, who is receptive to prayer for the land, keeping the plague away from Israel (v. 25). According to the narratives in Samuel–Kings, this is the only altar built by David. A new center of healing for the land emerges in Jerusalem.

David's affair with Bathsheba, the plot that results in the death of Uriah, the judgment of Nathan, the death of the first child born to Bathsheba and David, and the birth of Solomon are all found in 2 Samuel 11:1–12:25. The details are well known, so there is no need to rehearse them here. The narrative is notable for its gaps and ambiguities that require the reader to think about possibilities that are not explicitly stated. The matter of unfilled gaps is characteristic of many narratives, especially biblical ones.

In this story the gap/ambiguity is produced by the narrative's persistent use of external circumstances and avoidance of references to internal feelings, motives, and intentions. For example, we are not told what David's intent is when he sends for Bathsheba, who is described as "very beautiful." Is his purpose purely sexual? Is there also a political/social motivation? Bathsheba is said to be the daughter of Eliam and the wife of Uriah the Hittite, an unusually full designation of a woman's name. We know that Uriah is one of David's elite warriors, although his exact identity is hard to establish. He has a Yahwistic name ("Yahweh is my light"), and the "Hittite" designation may be an indication of ethnic identity (neo-Hittite/Aramaen) rather than an indication that he is a foreign mercenary. We know nothing about Eliam, but he may be one of David's elite warriors and a prominent citizen of Jerusalem. (He is listed as a son of Ahithophel, a chief counselor of David [2 Sam 23:24].)

We are told nothing of Bathsheba's feelings. Is she taken to David against her will? Is she willing to submit to the famous king and lover, or does she have a choice? Does she have any idea of what David wants before she goes to the palace? Is it possible that David is set up? (The Bible reader knows that she sends a message, "I am pregnant," in the same manner as Tamar sends a message to Judah in Gen 38:25). It is unclear who knows what. Clearly Bathsheba and David know she is pregnant (11:5), but who else knows? The messengers? Does Uriah know or suspect that David has had an affair with his wife? Does David know, or suspect, that Uriah knows? Why doesn't Uriah walk the short distance from David's palace to his house? Is he a true-blue idealist, fully committed to the ideals of holy war, or is he attempting to subvert David's power, maybe topple him from the throne and clear the way for someone else to be king (Joab?). What does Joab know? Why does he disobey David's order to leave Uriah exposed to meet his death, and instead includes Uriah with a number of "David's servants" who are killed in fighting near the city wall? Questions such as these are explored at considerable length in *The Poetics of Biblical Narrative* (Meir Sternberg), which has become a classic in Old Testament study. The reader is left to ponder possible answers.

Some things are clear, however. First, David's guilt is without question: "I have sinned against Yahweh" (12:13). The narrative establishes David's guilt by "sober recitation" of his actions and speech, whatever may be his inner thought or motivation. The positive characterization of David in the preceding chapters implodes with a shocking impact on the reader, at least until a closer look is taken at the preceding narratives. Thus we may notice such things as the arrogance of power in chapter 6, including David's treatment of Michal, the abortive proposal to build a temple in chapter 7, the brutal massacre of Moabites in 8:2, the acquisition of great wealth from defeated enemies, and the suspicion that political success motivates most of David's personal relationships, including his marriages.

Second, the multiple ironies in the narratives are clear. The beginning in 11:1-2 says that "when kings go out to battle" David sends Joab and the forces of Israel to battle while he "sits" in Jerusalem, lying on a couch for his afternoon siesta and arising to walk about the roof of the palace to look down on other roofs. Kings are expected to go to battle with their troops. But David is in his house, not in the camp with his army; walking about his roof in the cool of the day, not walking about where his soldiers are laying siege to Rabbah. David has become one of a long line of leaders who make war but send others to fight, going to the scene of action only to get the glory of victory (12:26-31). The Masoretic Hebrew text of 11:1 actually reads "when messengers go out to war," but the idea of kings seems primary (as in other Hebrew texts and the Greek text). However, there may be a play on words here: when a king like David does not go out to battle, messengers go back and forth and become involved in the action. Without the messengers, there would be no affair with Bathsheba and no death for Uriah.

When messengers start to run for kings, there is trouble, especially when one carries the first written order in the Bible.

Another irony is found in the contrast between David's reign as it is described in 8:15 and his conduct in chapter 11. In 8:15 he is said to administer "justice and equity for all the people." The contrast with this in chapter 11 requires no comment, as he plunders the wife of one of his best soldiers and arranges for his death in a battle far away. This is hardly "justice and righteousness for all his people." The contrast between Uriah's dedication to his leader and his fellow troops is striking when compared with David's attempt to hide his behavior and his cynical response to the message of Joab in 11:25: "Do not let this matter trouble you, for the sword devours now one and now another; press your attack."

Perhaps the greatest irony in the whole account is the seeming absence of Yahweh. David seems to be alone with all his power in Jerusalem, but he is not. Suddenly, in 11:27, we are told that the thing David has done displeases Yahweh"—more correctly, the thing was condemned by Yahweh. God has been there all along, watching the affair in Jerusalem! The divine absence only seems to be such—Yahweh knows the whole story (as does Nathan): "Why have you despised the word of the Lord to do what is evil in his sight?" (12:9a). Nothing is hidden from the eyes of God.

The account in 2 Samuel 12:1-23 has more than one unusual feature. First, Nathan's parable seems so contrived, it appears that David should have seen through it at once. Why does he reply in literal terms in verses 5-6? Possibly because to answer otherwise would be a confession of his sin. Or, should we understand David as being so warped in judgment that he fails to understand that in this context he has been stripped of moral authority and his impulsive oath to make the rich man pay four times for the stolen lamb is hollow? Does he consider himself free from judgment while meting it out to others? Further, Nathan's reply to David that "you are the man," is usually understood as David. But Polzin (122-26) points out that the referent of "the man" varies in the interpretation of the parable in 12:7-12. In verses 7-8, David is the traveler who comes to the rich man's house, having received the power and the "house" of Saul by the gift of Yahweh. He is the rich man who takes the family ewe from the poor man in verses 9-10 (having killed Uriah and taken his wife), but in verses 11-12 David will be the poor man who will dishonorably lose his wives.

Another feature of this narrative is David's grief prior to the death of his child. We expect such intense bereavement *after* the child's death; however, when it happens, David washes and anoints himself and goes to the house of Yahweh for worship, then returns to his own house and eats food (vv. 19-20). This is the surprising David, with a superb sense of timing and appropriate behavior. The cynical David of chapter 11 gives way to the David "after Yahweh's heart," with wisdom and theological insight. David moves from the shadow of death into the realm of new life, ready to leave the past behind and move toward the future. This is a bright spot in the dark tapestry of the history of his life in chapters 11–20.

David's statement about the death of the child in 12:23 has been much remembered: "Can I bring him back again? I shall go to him, but he will not return to me." We do not know what individual Israelites thought about life after death, but in the general context of the Old Testament, David's words would only mean that he would join the child in death, but the child would not live again. However, Christians can hardly read the statement without hearing it in the context of the resurrection that is inseparably linked with the resurrection of Jesus Christ (1 Cor 15:12-19). The Christian should not read resurrection backwards into the text, but the text moves forward into the "living hope" of those who are in Christ (1 Pet 1:3-5).

A final irony in this account is the birth of David's successor out of the sordid affair. Bathsheba names the child Solomon, which is traditionally associated with *shalom*, meaning "peace or well-being," although it could mean "his replacement," either for Uriah or for the first child who died. However, Nathan gives him the name Jedidah, "beloved of Yahweh," as assurance of the divine favor of Yahweh. The divine grace moves on, amazing and undeterred by human folly. We can hardly avoid a mixture of fascination and revulsion in the accounts of Samuel, Saul, and David. The good and the bad are blended together in a way that rejects easy conclusions. Israel, the people of Yahweh, is embodied in these three persons as much as in Abraham, Jacob, and Moses. The ways of God are beyond our understanding.

III. The temple

A. Economic and political aspects

Temples were integral parts of urban economy in the ancient world, and there is no need to conclude otherwise for the Jerusalem Temple. Characteristically, temples owned large estates of land, with grain fields, groves, and flocks to provide for support and offerings. However, ownership of temple land seems to be lacking for the Israelite Temple. Yahweh owns *all* the land in Yahwistic theology, and gifts and offerings are expected from the people who live on the land as tenants allowed by Yahweh to use it.

Temples provided employment for considerable numbers of people: priests, attendants, helpers, and those who engaged in temple business. Temples also seem to have functioned as distribution centers and even as manufacturing centers, where cloth and other products were made for trade. Although the Old Testament texts are not specific, it is reasonable to assume that a three-tiered complex of rooms, surrounding the temple on three sides, known as "chambers" or "side rooms," was the location of the temple treasury and served as the storehouse of gold and other precious items. In brief, the temple was a major repository of national wealth.

The economic function of temples also included the provision of services designed to restore the ill, using therapeutic healing procedures of various sorts, with religious aspects—for example, thanksgiving services for those who had regained their health. The most famous of healing temples is the Asclepius temple at Epidaurus in Greece in the fourth century BCE, but such temple centers of healing are also known from Mesopotamia. Gifts were brought to these temples by those seeking healing, and there are indications that fees were charged.

A temple, which served as a residence for the god of the king and his people, was an effective way of communicating the god's favor on the sponsoring reign. In the case of the Davidic monarchy, the idea of Yahweh's covenant with David and the movement of the ark to a tent in

Jerusalem, along with the erection of an altar on the threshing floor of Araunah, had already legitimized the kingship in terms of past traditions, but the temple of Solomon moved it to a new level, and it became an integral part of the formation of the monarchical state. The political importance of the temple is evident in Jeroboam's swift moves to establish worship centers at Bethel and Dan in the newly formed northern kingdom, despite the weakness of two centers versus one.

B. The house of God

The English word for temple (derived from the Latin *templum*, a "consecrated spot," or a "sanctuary") is used to translate the Hebrew *hekal*, which has its roots in the concept of a "great house," a large building or a palace that can be used as a residence for a deity or a king. In biblical texts the terms *bet* Yahweh or *bet 'elohim*, "house of Yahweh" and "house of God," are far more common than "temple." The "house" of a deity is considered to be the earthly residence of the deity. In 1 Kings 8 this concept is modified so that its physical nature is not equated directly with the full presence of God. Solomon declares in 8:13 "I have built you an exalted house, a place for you to dwell in forever," but in the following verses there is a repeated emphasis on the name of Yahweh in the house, while prayers are answered from heaven. In verse 27 Solomon declares: "But will God indeed dwell on the earth? Even heaven and the highest heaven cannot contain you, much less this house that I have built!" Nevertheless, the temple is a place of concentrated and effective divine presence.

The divine presence means that the temple is an intensely sacred space, holy and separate from the ordinary world. The temple structure itself expressed a separation between the holiness of God and human beings, with laypersons allowed to enter only into the courts of the temple. The thick walls and the gradations of holiness from the entrance to the holy of holies protected the holy core of the divine presence, which is conceptualized as almost a physical entity with great, even lethal, power.

The temple in Jerusalem incorporates the holiness of Yahweh in a focused and concentrated form, a holiness that pervades the whole earth, as when Isaiah hears the heavenly chorus declare: "Holy, holy, holy is the Lord of Hosts; the whole earth is full of his glory"(Isa 6:3). Thus, temple theology is basically creation theology, so that the temple becomes a microcosm of creation, an expression in stone, wood, gold, and exquisite decorations as a testimony to Yahweh's creatorship of the cosmic order. The temple imagery is designed to set forth creation theology, as in the great laver (large cleansing basin) and the elaborate floral and fauna motifs in the carvings and decorations of the interior of the temple. Also, the seven years of building the Temple correlate with the seven days of creation (Gen 1).

C. Zionism

The temple in Jerusalem was built on a low hill called Mount Zion. Zion appears sometimes as another name for Jerusalem. The ideology of the cosmic mountain is frequently associated with temples, and this is the case with the temple in Jerusalem. The cosmic mountain, with a temple on top, functioned as an Axis Mundi, the axis forming a junction between the realms of the heavens, the earth, and the netherworld.

In ancient thought, the meeting place of the gods was on a cosmic mountain, which was also the epicenter of conflicting forces, divine, human, and nonhuman. Thus it was the power center of the world and the communicative medium between heaven and earth.

Temples were architecturally replicated embodiments of primitive cosmic mountains designed to represent the center of the world and the line of intercourse between realms of heaven, earth, and the netherworld. The role of Zion and the temple as the cosmic mountain center of the world, chosen by Yahweh for a habitation, is confirmed by Old Testament texts. Examples include Psalm 48:1-2, which speaks of "the city of the great King." "beautiful in elevation," "the joy of all the earth," "in the far north." The cosmic mountain extends to the highest heavens, into the

realm of clouds and stars, but its base goes down into the
lowest depths of the abyss of the netherworld. The mountain of the temple is to be established as the highest of the
mountains, raised above the hills, and all nations and
peoples will flow to it (Isa 2:2-3; Mic 4:1-23; cf. Ezek 40:2).

The fusion of the heavenly habitation of Yahweh and
the temple is easy to understand against the background of
the cosmic mountain. Thus prayer is made on earth, but
the response of Yahweh comes from the heavenly realm (2
Sam 22; Ps 18), where the king's cry on earth is heard in
Yahweh's heavenly temple, from whence he descends with
great power to deliver. Psalm 11:4 sets forth Yahweh as
being on his heavenly throne and in the temple at the same
time: "Yahweh is in his holy temple; Yahweh's throne is in
heaven." Yahweh's presence in the temple on Mount Zion
does not mean that he is absent from the heavenly throne.
The temple context is transfigured for the prophet in
Isaiah 6:1-8, who sees Yahweh "sitting on a throne, high
and lofty," while the "hem of his robe" descends into the
temple to fill it. The physical reality of the temple merges
into the spiritual reality it embodies.

When the theology of the Zion-temple merged with
royal ideology, a powerful mix of Zion tradition—which I
call "Zionism"—resulted. Zion is the place where Yahweh
establishes the king as a son of God (Ps 2). Zion is Yahweh's chosen habitation, His "resting place forever," and
the place where he will "cause a horn to sprout up for
David" (Ps 132:13-17). In the traditions of the exodus and
wilderness experiences, Yahweh is said to go forth from
Sinai/Horeb or from Teman and the mountain country of
Paran (Deut 33:2), but in Psalm 50:1-3 Yahweh "shines
forth" from Zion, "the perfection of beauty," and comes
forth with devouring fire and a mighty tempest. Zion, not
Sinai, is now the locus of Yahweh's power and strength.

Zionism received strength from two other aspects of
temple life. First, the great festivals conducted in the
temple area strengthened the grip of the temple and its personnel on religious life. Zion is said to be "the city of our
appointed festivals" (Isa 33:20). Jeroboam understood the
significance of the autumn festival when he appointed a

rival festival to offset the festival in Jerusalem. The festivals, of course, were usually joyous occasions for those who participated. The speaker in Psalm 122:1 doubtless speaks for many who went to Jerusalem for the festivals: "I was glad when they said to me, 'Let us go to the house of the Lord.' " The temple was designed to be a paradise-like replica of the Garden of Eden, described in Ezekiel 28:11-15 as the "garden of God" or "the holy mountain of God." Festival-goers would be taught the theology and ideology of Zionism, and the splendor of the surroundings in the midst of the royal court and power undoubtedly stamped them with lasting impressions passed to others (Ps 48:12-14).

We can easily recognize far-reaching changes in worship and religious life from that associated with family, tribal, and community worship. The temple and its attendant royal establishment transformed Yahwism into the official religion of the state. We should guard against the conclusion that official religion is necessarily worse than the personal piety of family-based religion. Family-based piety is susceptible to private interpretations of all sorts. It lacks the teaching capacity and the strength of the standardization of official religion. The temple has its merits and its dangers; religious life needs both.

A second auxiliary factor in the strength of Zionism was the development of the ideology of the inviolability of Zion-Jerusalem, as seen for example in Psalm 46. The nations will be defeated before Zion, their weapons destroyed, and their raging put down. This concept receives strong reinforcement by the deliverance of Jerusalem from the Assyrians in 701 BCE, as reflected in 2 Kings 18:13-19:37 and Isaiah 36:1-37:38.

D. Temple and tent

Zionism is not the whole story of the temple. From its beginning, the temple generated theological resistance and revision of the common temple ideology of the ancient Near East in terms of the theological tenets of Yahwism. One modification moved along the lines of the old tent tradition of Yahweh worship. As already noted in the account of the dedication of the temple in 1 Kings 8:1-11, the ark of the covenant of Yahweh and the tent of meeting, along with the holy vessels in the tent, were brought to the temple, with the ark being put in the inner sanctuary of the temple.

The ark, of course, was associated with the wilderness period of Israel's history, a sign of God's presence and guidance of the people from Sinai/Horeb to the promised land. The placement of the ark in the inner sanctuary was such that the poles used to carry it protruded out so that they were visible in the holy place, but not on the outside of the temple. The ark and its carrying poles stressed the linkage of Yahweh with Israel by covenant at Sinai/Horeb, not with David, and symbolized the mobile nature of Yahweh's presence. Also, the ark was empty except for the two tables of stone put in it by Moses at Horeb.

Another feature of the account in 1 Kings 8:1-11 that connects the temple to the wilderness traditions is the cloud that fills the temple with the glory of Yahweh, so much so that the priests cannot stand to minister. The cloud guided the Israelites in the wilderness and stood either above or at the entrance of the ten of meeting to bring messages to Moses and the people. Commentators tend to treat verse 4 as a gloss, and they discount the movement of the tent of meeting to, or into, the temple. There is really no good reason for doing so, however, and the installation of the tent sanctuary in the temple along with the ark and the "holy vessels" in the tent is probable.

Although the textual evidence is not direct, it is also probable that David's tent for the ark was, or became in time, an elaborate tent sanctuary that served in place of a temple until Solomon built the Temple at Jerusalem. The equipment was elaborate. Note the following references: "in a tent and a tabernacle" (2 Sam 7:6); "horn of oil from the tent" brought out by Zadok to anoint Solomon (1 Kgs 1:39); "holy vessels" in the tent of meeting (1 Kgs 8:4); and the things David had dedicated, "the silver, the gold, and the vessels" brought to the temple and stored in the treasury rooms (7:51). All this hardly points to the equipment of a simple tent shrine.

In addition, David appoints Levites to serve with song at the "tabernacle of the tent of meeting" until Solomon builds the Temple (1 Chron 6:31-32), which indicates more than a simple tent shrine. The reference to David going "into the house of the Lord" (2 Sam 12:20) is strange and may be an anachronism, but the interplay between tent-tabernacle and temple seems informative. The structure at Shiloh is called a "temple" (1 Sam 1:9; 3:3), but it is also called a "house of God" (1 Sam 1:24) and the "tent of meeting" (1 Sam 2:22). It seems reasonable to conclude that David constructed an elaborate tent sanctuary on the threshing floor of Araunah in Jerusalem (see 2 Sam 24:24-25) where he also built an altar. At least, this seems to be as good, or better, than the theory that David took over a preexisting Jebusite temple on the threshing floor, and that Solomon's temple was actually a rebuilding and renovation of the Jebusite structure.

The tent tradition is deeply embedded in Pentateuchal narratives (see Exod 18; 33:7-11; Num 11:16-25; 12:1-16). The account in Exodus 33:7-11 is especially interesting. We read that Moses would pitch the "tent of meeting" outside the camp and then go to the tent, while the people watched from the entrances of their own tents, to meet with Yahweh who would "speak to Moses face to face." The presence of Yahweh was marked by a pillar of cloud standing at the entrance of the tent. An added detail is that Joshua stayed in the tent, even when Moses went back to the camp. The term "tent of meeting" refers to a tent designated as a place of meeting with Yahweh (ex: a mountain), thus a "tent of presence," but not presence as a constant, static reality, but a presence that changes from time to time. The tent of meeting seems relatively simple, easily pitched without many personnel (only Joshua in Exod 33:11), and was a shrine for receiving oracles from Yahweh. Thus, the tradition of a portable tent shrine in the wilderness is found along with the ark. Indeed, the tent and the ark seem to have been separate from one another in the earliest traditions.

The correlation of the temple with the tent and ark traditions had two major effects. On the one hand, Zionism was strengthened by the Deuteronomic insistence on worship at one chosen place—the temple. This emphasis is found also in the priestly material and Chronicles. Zion is the "place," chosen by Yahweh for His king and for His people to worship. In this respect, Sinai has been superseded by Zion. On the other hand, the royal ideology and the creation theology of Zionism have been merged into the theology of Moses, the covenant of Sinai, and the wilderness traditions; that is, the theology of exodus, guidance, and gift of land to the people (not to the king). Yahweh, who shines forth from Zion, is the divine warrior who delivered His people from Egypt and thrust out other peoples to give them their land.

IV. Wisdom

Wisdom in the Bible encompasses a sizeable cluster of words: understanding, wise dealing, shrewdness, prudence, learning, discerning (Prov 1:2-7). The "fear of the Lord" is also used to describe wisdom. The basic idea of wisdom is that of the ability to get something done well. As such, wisdom may be used for the practical skill of an artisan. Also, coping with life situations is a mark of wisdom, for example, the small but wise animals and the act of steering a right course through life.

Wisdom is deeply rooted in the experience of life, human and nonhuman. It emerges from observation, reflection, and listening to the understanding of others. One must seek wisdom, but in the final analysis wisdom is always the gift of God. The truly wise are those endowed by divine charisma. Thus, Solomon asks Yahweh for "an understanding mind" and the ability to "discern between good and evil," and the skill to "govern your people" (1 Kgs 3:9). It pleases Yahweh to grant Solomon's request: "I give you a wise and discerning mind" (v. 12).

One of the primary sources for wisdom in the ancient Near East was the royal court. The king or queen, along with his/her counselors and scribes, was expected to be skilled in wisdom sayings and techniques. The wisdom literature and the Solomonic narratives have an international character and reflect the intercourse in wisdom among the courts of the ancient world.

The emphasis on wisdom in relation to Solomon provokes the question of the role of wisdom thought and theology in Joshua–Kings. Two features of wisdom thought seem to emerge. First, the presence and action of God are characteristically veiled or hidden in the wisdom literature. The direct presence and active interventions of Yahweh in the Pentateuch and in some sections of DH are missing in the wisdom literature. There is no exodus, no leading and protecting of the people in the wilderness, no crossing of the Jordan, no possession of the land by taking it from the Canaanites. On the other hand, the lack of visible engagement of Yahweh in great "acts of God" does not mean that God has disappeared. There is a hidden presence that works its way through human life and events, leaving human beings to operate out of a divine endowment of wisdom. Yahweh guarantees that the order and interconnectedness of all creation works, but leaves the implementation to human efforts, at least on the surface of things.

In the account of Solomon's reign, he is endowed with wisdom as the gift of God. This is made clear in 1 Kings 3, 4, and 5. However, Solomon carries out the organization of his kingdom and his building projects (temple and palace complex) with almost no explicit divine direction or help. His divine commission to build the temple is confirmed, not by an oracle from Yahweh, but by a letter from King Hiram of Tyre. Solomon relies on the wisdom of Hiram, a master-craftsman. Solomon's initial declaration regarding the temple is: "I have built you [the Lord] an exalted house, a place for you to dwell in forever" (8:13). Solomon's building projects were carried out in terms of all he desired to build, not what Yahweh wanted him to build. In other words, Solomon operated on his own, supposedly out of the wisdom given to him by Yahweh.

The second aspect of wisdom in the account of Solomon's reign reflects the equation of wisdom with obedience to the commandments of Yahweh. In Deuteronomy 4:6-7 Moses exhorts the Israelites about to enter the land to obey the commandments of Yahweh: "for this will show your wisdom and discernment in the sight of the peoples." The people who observe the Israelites' faithfulness will declare that this is a "wise and discerning people."

The word of Yahweh comes to Solomon in 1 Kings 6:11-13 concerning his need to keep the commandments of Yahweh as a condition of the promise made to David about the temple and the commitment of Yahweh to dwell among "my people Israel." The expression "this house that you are building" is emphatic; the temple is being built out of Solomon's wisdom, but the success of that wisdom depends upon the *torah* of Yahweh. Wisdom must be supplemented by obedience (see 9:1-9). Otherwise, the temple will become a "heap of ruins" and evoke "hissing" from those who pass by it.

When the final summary of Solomon's reign is given (1 Kgs 11:1-39), there is not a word about his wisdom. Negative judgment streams through the summary, and wisdom has disappeared. The glory of diplomatic and economic wisdom and success, even when the wisdom is divinely given, does not stay the judgment for disobedience to Yahweh, especially in going after "other gods," with his "heart turned away from the Lord, the God of Israel, who had appeared to him twice" (v. 9). In the final analysis, was Solomon a wise man or a fool? He was both, of course—a wise man who became a fool.

V. Prophets and prophecy

Prophets and prophecy become prolific with the end of the reign of Solomon. Among the prophets listed in Kings are: Ahijah, Shemaiah, unnamed prophets from Judah and Bethel, Elijah, and Elisha. Their speeches constitute a significant part of the content of the narratives in Kings. The fulfillment of previous prophecy is repeatedly noted. The time span is usually relatively short (1 Kgs 11:31-39; 12:15), but it may be extended, as in the case of the altar at Bethel (1 Kgs 13:1-10; 2 Kgs 23:15-16). Ahijah during the time of Jeroboam (930–909 BCE) foretells the exile of the northern kingdom ca. 722 BCE. The destruction of Judah and Jerusalem (2 Kgs 20–24) is the subject of several prophets: Isaiah, Huldah, the narrator, and an unnamed prophet.

Of course, the fall of Judah and Jerusalem is the topic of major sections of the prophetic books other than Joshua–Kings. The Deuteronomistic thesis in Samuel–Kings is that Yahweh allows a great deal of flux and flow to human affairs, but the final control and management of history belong to the divine will, marked by the divine word delivered by the prophets. The history of the kings is also the history of the prophets, who bring to bear the judgments of the King, Yahweh, on their reigns. The title of the book of Kings might well be that of the book of Kings and Prophets.

Discussions of prophecy in the Old Testament have had a tendency to move toward one or the other of two overemphases. On the one hand, prophecy has been treated as mainly pure prediction, with little attention given to the messages of the prophets about justice, righteousness, and religious practice. On the other hand, an overemphasis on the prophets as speakers dealing with ethical, social, and religious issues of their own time has obscured their role as "foretellers," concerned with what God is going to do in the future. The truth of the matter is that the prophets appear as both "forthtellers" and "foretellers."

The partial fulfillment of prophetic hopes and the nature of some prophetic writing may bother modern commentators and readers but do not seem to have troubled the biblical writers. The poise of the biblical writers in the face of what seem to be delays, defaults, or contradictions in fulfillments should warn us not to attempt the forced harmonizing, which has been done so often. For example, Joshua 21:43-45 says that all the land Yahweh had promised to the Israelites was possessed by them by the end of Joshua's work, whereas the book of Judges opens with an account of tribal efforts to conquer and settle the land, and there is no sign of embarrassment or apology for the inconsistency. A similar situation is provoked by the high expectations of a return of the Israelites from exile in Isaiah 40–66 and the very limited extent of the return as recorded in Ezra–Nehemiah. The glowing promises of Isaiah are not harmonized with or adjusted to the limited realities of the return and the continuation of exile. One factor here is the usually generalized language by the prophets about the future. The true nature and validity of a prophecy become evident only in fulfillment in some event.

New Testament scholars are accustomed to this phenomenon in regard to the work of Jesus Christ. For example, in Matthew, Jesus' disciples are taught to pray for the kingdom to come, even though Jesus begins his preaching ministry with the message given earlier by John the Baptist: "Repent, for the kingdom of heaven has come near" (3:2), and the kingdom is said to be present (12:28) and will reach its culmination in the generation of the disciples of Jesus (16:28; 24:34). This is, of course, is an example of what is frequently called the "delayed parousia" (the full manifestation of the power of Christ, commonly referred to as the second coming). There is, however, no sense of crisis in the New Testament (with the possible exception of 2 Pet 3:3-10) or the early church about the deferment of the completion of the work of Christ. The falling short of expressed hope seems to reflect an acceptance of the nature of prophecy as living tradition always moving toward a new fulfillment. The work of God is never fully finished within the ken of human beings, and prophetic words are always alive.

Conclusion

From promise to exile: how did the chosen people, the treasure of God, go from promise to oppression by foreigners, from inhabitants of a land of milk and honey to a landless people? The exodus and the exile are the two great poles in the faith history of Israel. The exodus from Egypt was the great saving act of Yahweh to which Israel looked back. The exile, however, is the context for hammering out the theology of Yahwism and the formation of most of the Old Testament. For a minority of the Israelites, the exile ended after 539 BCE when they returned to Jerusalem, reestablished community life, and rebuilt the temple. However, many others remained in faraway places, and their numbers increased with the passing years. At the end of the book of Kings, large numbers of Israelites (northern and southern) have been deported to Babylon, but some have made a journey into exile in Egypt. And even for those who returned to Jerusalem, the exile was not really over.

Those who did not return to Palestine were unlikely to have given up the idea of exile simply because Cyrus and the Persians allowed others to go back to Jerusalem. On the contrary, they probably used the idea of exile and the return of some to justify their own reluctance, or inability, to uproot themselves from their living places and make a hazardous move to Judah, where they would live among hostile strangers and poor economic conditions. In the centuries that followed, Israelites always lived under the domination of great powers, never knowing what it was to be really free—Babylonians, Persians, Greeks, Romans. Exile became a way of life and thought. The continuing emphasis in Israelite-Jewish life on the motifs of a return from exile to Jerusalem and the restoration of Israel testifies clearly that in theological thought the exile did not end with the return of some Jews to Jerusalem. A postexilic prayer of Ezra expresses the reality of continuing exile:

> Here we are, slaves to this day—slaves in the land that you gave to our ancestors to enjoy its fruit and its good gifts. Its rich yield goes to the kings whom you have set over us because of our sins; they have power over our bodies and over our livestock at their pleasure, and we are in great distress. (Neh 9:36-37)

Some of the people returned to the land, but the "exile" of oppression from foreign kings and only partial restoration remained.

There was a prophetic expectation of a future deliverance that would take the form of a new and more wonderful exodus and would dwarf the partial endings of exile already known. But an extended exile must be traversed before the new time of Yahweh would come. For example, in the book of Daniel the seventy-year exile of Jeremiah is extended to "seventy weeks," taken to mean seventy weeks of years, and the end is not yet. The book ends with two extensions of time (1290 days in 12:11 and 1335 days in 12:12), and the "end" has not yet come. The message of the book seems rather clear: the Israelites in exile should live like Daniel and his companions (chs. 1–6), even in times of terrible oppression (chs. 7–12), faithful unto death if necessary because the "end" will come and there will be a resurrection for those whose names are "written in the book." The end is not yet; the seventy years are not yet fulfilled, but the end is decreed and will not be stopped by any earthly power.

Another indication of a prolonged sense of exile is found in the fact that the Pentateuch ends with the death of Moses and without the fulfillment of the promise of the land. The story line in the Pentateuch extends into the land, anticipating a future when the Israelites will be there, but they are only at the border when Deuteronomy closes. The promise of Yahweh has not yet found its intended fulfillment when we meet the Israelites in the book of Joshua. Joshua–Kings, of course, moves from land to exile. As a result, the Pentateuch becomes a great manual of instruction for exiles who live out of the promise of God for the future, in unresolved hope and a lack of closure.

N. T. Wright (*The New Testament and the People of God; Jesus and the Victory of God*) argues forcefully for the "end of exile" as a basic element ("a shorthand") for the expectation that Yahweh would act in Israel's history and bring a new era. The New Testament gathers the work of Jesus, the Messiah of Israel, around and within this expectation. The ending of the exile is focused on Jesus Christ and his ministry. Even in Christ, however, we wait for the full end of the exile, for a further coming, for the New Jerusalem to come down out of heaven to a new heaven and a new earth. Meanwhile, we live with the assurance that what has begun so powerfully in Jesus Christ will be completed. We shall not be disappointed, as we look from afar to "the city that has foundations, whose architect and builder is God" (Heb 11:10). In a sense, all of God's people live in exile, waiting for the fulfillment of the promise of God to live in His presence. From promise to exile, yes, but also from exile into promise.

For Further Reading

Anderson, A. A. *2 Samuel*. Word Biblical Commentary. Dallas: Word, 1989.

Auld, A. Graeme. *I & II Kings*. The Daily Study Bible Series. Philadelphia: Westminster, 1986.

Birch, Bruce C. "The First and Second Books of Samuel." *The New Interpreter's Bible*. Edited by Leander E. Keck, et. al., 949–1383. Volume 2. Nashville: Abingdon, 1998.

Brueggemann, Walter. *First and Second Kings*. Interpretation. Louisville KY: John Knox, 1990.

Cogan, Mordechai, and Hayim Tadmor. *II Kings*. The Anchor Bible. New York: Doubleday, 1988.

Fokkelman, J. P. *The Narrative Art and Poetry in the Books of Samuel*. 4 vols.: I, "King David," 1981; II, "The Crossing Fates," 1986; III, "Throne and City," 1990; IV, "Vow and Desire," 1993. Assen-Maastricht, The Netherlands: Van Gorcum.

Gray, John. *I and II Kings*, 2d ed. The Old Testament Library. Philadelphia: Westminster, 1970.

Grizzard, Carol Stuart. "First and Second Samuel." *Mercer Commentary on the Bible*. Edited by Watson E. Mills, et al., 269-301. Macon GA: Mercer University Press, 1990.

Hackett, Jo Ann. "1 and 2 Samuel." *The Women's Bible Commentary*. Edited by Carol A. Newsom and Sharon H. Ringe, 85-95. Louisville KY: Westminster/John Knox, 1992.

Hobbs, T. R. *2 Kings*. Word Biblical Commentary. Waco TX: Word, 1985.

House, Paul R. *1, 2 Kings*. The New American Commentary. Nashville: Broadman & Holman, 1995.

Klein, Ralph W. *1 Samuel*. Word Biblical Commentary. Waco TX: Word, 1983.

McCarter, Jr., P. Kyle. *I Samuel*. The Anchor Bible. New York: Doubleday, 1980.

_____. *II Samuel*. The Anchor Bible. New York: Doubleday, 1984.

Nelson, Richard D. *First and Second Kings*. Atlanta: John Knox, 1987.

Polzin, Robert. *Samuel and the Deuteronomist*. 1 Samuel. San Francisco: Harper & Row, 1989.

_____. *David and the Deuteronomist*. 2 Samuel. Bloomington IA: Indiana University Press, 1993.

Rosenberg, Joel. "1 and 2 Samuel." *The Literary Guide to the Bible*. Edited by Robert Alter and Frank Kermode, 122-43. Cambridge MA: Belknap University Press, 1987.

Smothers, Thomas G. "First and Second Kings." *Mercer Commentary on the Bible*. Edited by Watson Mills, et. al., 303-22. Macon GA: Mercer University Press, 1990.

Walsh, Jerome T. *1 Kings*. Berit Olam. Collegeville MN: Liturgical Press, 1996.

ALL THE BIBLE

ALL THE BIBLE SERIES DESCRIPTION

AREA	TITLE*
Genesis–Deuteronomy	*Journey to the Land of Promise*
Former Prophets	*From Promise to Exile*
Latter Prophets, excluding Postexilic	*God's Servants, the Prophets*
Poetry, Wisdom Literature	*The Testimony of Poets and Sages*
Exilic, Postexilic Books	*The Exile and Beyond*
The Four Gospels	*The Church's Portraits of Jesus*
Acts of the Apostles, Epistles of Paul	*The Church's Mission to the Gentiles*
Hebrews–Revelation	*The Church as a Pilgrim People*

*subject to change